Scene Scripts Three

LONGMAN IMPRINT BOOKS

Scene Scripts Three

a third selection of television plays,
from the BBC Schools TV series, *Scene*,
by

David Hopkins
Jack Ronder
David Cook
Leonard Kingston

edited by
Roy Blatchford, MA
Pimlico School, London

Longman

LONGMAN GROUP LIMITED
Longman House
Burnt Mill, Harlow, Essex CM20 2JE, England
and Associated Companies throughout the World.

First published by arrangement with the British Broadcasting Corporation 1982
Third impression 1983
ISBN 0 582 22309 1

Set in Baskerville 10/11 (Linotron 202)

Printed in Hong Kong
by Astros Printing Ltd

Contents

Introduction

This is the third Imprint volume of playscripts taken from the BBC television's schools programme *Scene*, a long-running series which brings together a varied and thought-provoking mixture of plays and documentaries centred on contemporary social issues. In common with the two previous collections, *Scene Scripts Three* contains a group of plays which are first and foremost entertaining and enjoyable to read through or act out, but which are also certain to prompt teenagers into discussing questions raised in the dramas which touch closely on their own lives. The essential subject matter of the plays may seem rather bleak and depressing, yet at the same time they include scenes of lively humour and unexpected action, bold characterisation and brisk dialogue, and interesting storylines with which, at odd moments, we might identify.

What the four plays have in common is their focus on incidents and personal experiences familiar to our everyday lives at home, school or work: parents and children who seem unable to understand one another's points of view; children as victims of family turmoil; adults living together who discover irreconcilable tensions breaking them apart; one individual being threatened and bullied by others; adolescents having to face up to the consequences of their actions; people coming to terms with grief, even death. It is the working out of these situations in dramatic terms that lies at the heart of the *Scene Scripts Three* collection. While we might not always agree with the solution offered or sympathise with one character's course of action, at least we are challenged into thinking a little more deeply about our own feelings, actions and decisions in real life.

Good drama seeks to educate as well as entertain; it affords the opportunity for an audience to bring into balance their own lives and the pressures of the times. The strength of these four plays is that the writers have constructed their drama in such a way that we witness events through the eyes of different characters and are thus implicitly invited to take sides. Throughout the plays we are constantly being asked to examine our own attitudes and assumptions in relation to those of the characters. We are being asked: What course of action would we have followed in the same circumstances? Who is to blame? Who do we empathise with and why?

In the first play, *Coins Against the Wall*, David's parents are seen to be over-protective and insensitive to his inner feelings, a fact which leads to his being exploited by the school bullies. The play raises inevitable questions about what parents and children expect of one another, about teachers' awareness of young people's problems, about bullying as an inescapable fact of life. The headmaster deals with the bullies in one way; is it effective, or would we have resolved David's anxieties differently?

It is another disturbing fact of life that more and more marriages end in divorce and separation; in *The Kids are Okay* we watch this painful process of separation within one family and rapidly discover that the children, Jill and Kenny, are far from "Okay". Indeed Jill resorts to extreme measures as a cry for help, and even at the climax of the drama we are left wondering whether anything has been learned. Similar cries for help are sounded in *If Only*, a moving play which examines something nearly all of us have to face at some stage in our lives: the loss of someone close to us. Brian is profoundly affected by his best friend's tragic death but appears to receive little sympathy from those closest to him. In turn, Mrs Thompson's grief is desperate to the point of violence. Once again, we are tempted to ask, *if only* someone had responded a little differently then personal pain might have been partially mitigated.

As the title of the fourth play might suggest, its two central characters have to learn to live with the problematic *consequences* of their actions. Paul and Liza find themselves isolated and pitched against the wishes of their stubborn parents – a classic and explosive example of the generation gap. Leonard Kingston's portrayal of two families in emotional turmoil is a powerfully cast and convincing drama, enjoyable to read and worthy of close study.

All four plays were of course first conceived in visual terms and have been very slightly adapted for classroom reading. Many of the original stage and studio directions have been edited to give a "cleaner" drama text, but this should in no way prevent those interested in television as a medium exploring the plays as a way of approaching a fuller understanding of television dramas; the points for discussion on pages 102–11 are intended to encourage this kind of wider study. The real merit of the scripts is that they lend themselves equally to reading around the class, improvisation, group discussion, theatre project work and to stage productions. In passing, perhaps they may also shed some light on our own family scenes.

Roy Blatchford

Writing *Consequences*

by Leonard Kingston

One morning the director, Andrée Molyneux, rang me to ask would I write a two-part 60-minute play for her about – well, a boy and a girl, and a pregnancy. It started as simply as that.

True, this hadn't come completely out of the blue. Some weeks before Andrée had trekked out to my place in Peckham to discuss the general idea. She had talked about the romantic notion that love is all, about plays where boy meets girl and they toddle off into the sunset together, happy ever after – and what rubbish all that was. Important to dig deeper, she said. She wasn't in the business of selling dreams on *Scene*. She wanted a realistic play about a real, believable love affair and what can happen to it, how it could go wrong, how it might break under strain. I had agreed with her, discussed possible writers – and more or less forgotten about it. I had other work on hand. Now I was agreeing to come up with this unromantic romantic play affair, and immediately beginning to worry. Could I deliver? Where was the story to come from? Who exactly was I to write about?

Starting

You're probably asking, why the worry? A love affair, a boy and girl, their families, a bit of uproar over the pregnancy – what's difficult about that? No, it sounds easy enough. But the problem I faced was *what* "boy and girl"? *what* "families"? A writer has to write about *real* people, individual people – real to *him*, I mean – and I had no real people in my head to latch this story on to. Without that, I would be writing with no enthusiasm, or involvement. It would be dead. Of course, it's different when you're writing for yourself, starting out on a project of your own. Then you have the characters forcing themselves upon you, the ideas are there already in your head. This was more like being sat down in a classroom and told to write an essay on – what? – An Exciting Experience, Love. Or so on. You just sit and stare at the blank sheets of paper, and pray. Which was, more or less, what I began doing. Staring, doodling, restlessly mooching around – yes, and praying, I suppose. The date when the script was due to be delivered was not far ahead. In fact, because of some re-scheduling of studio dates, the time available was much shorter than normal. I *had* to get started.

Then – I can't remember now exactly how or when an idea came. A small glimmer of excitement for me. I turned it over in my head. Yes, I could make something of this. Yet all that had occurred to me was something as ordinary and familiar as the thought of myself and my own family. Hardly sounds worth celebrating! But I had also remembered an incident from a few months or so before – of myself lazing in front of the tele, being startled by the ceiling shaking above my head, rushing upstairs to find my eldest daughter and a school friend bounding about in an amazing series of leaps and twirls. Rehearsing for their school gymnastics team, just as in the opening of the play as it now is. I was sent downstairs again to resume my tele-watching (as best I could) and that had been that. But my son had probably been in his room, next to my daughter's room, studying for his exams, reading – even asleep, perhaps – but certainly drowning out the commotion with his Mike Oldfield and "progressive" rock. In the next room was a small snooker table I had bought some years before in a fit of absentmindedness. So here were three teenagers (and a snooker table), all in close conjunction. The school friend was fairly attractive, but, as far I knew, my son had scarcely noticed her. What if he had? What if she'd been forced upon his notice? And if they were both a year or so older . . .?

Well, that basically was it. Now the people and the story began to come together in my head. I had a start. A father a little like myself – not too well in touch with his son (but how many fathers are?), short-tempered, possessive about his snooker table, a bit of a blusterer. A son, the boy, not completely different from my own son–shy, awkward, a bit vulnerable, perhaps. A daughter, again just a little like mine, cheeky, energetic. And, of course, the school friend – partly the real school friend, but more a combination of some of the young girls I knew at the school where I was teaching at that time, idealistic, loving, witty, but also tough and full of courage (they needed to be!). I wanted now a mother for the family. My own wife, Jen, would not do at all as a model – she would have been totally on the lovers' side, and that wasn't the way I felt this mother ought to be. She needed to be more highly strung, more neurotic, snobbish, perhaps – that would help create tension. I could think of several women like that – no problem imagining her. And with such a mother, the family immediately became more middle-class, and she probably hating the working-class district in which the family live (my district, of course, because now the scene was firmly set in South London). There were only two more characters I required – the girl's mum and dad – but I didn't have to bother about them for the moment. I had my theme, I had my people for the first scene. Now I could start.

Stopping for a moment

It may sound cold-blooded, the way I talk about constructing characters, as if I build them brick by brick, calculating each element – a bit of shyness here, a dab of cheeriness there. But, of course, I'm simplifying the process for the sake of convenience. Once you get a start, the characters start flooding in on you in a buzzing confusion of ideas, feelings, unconscious memories of people you have known, words – yes, even lines they would speak – these all coagulate together in the construction of characters. Probably half a dozen teachers – apart from myself – went in the making of the father. And characters provoke other characters, because I was telling a lie in leaving out the girl's mum and dad. In thinking of the girl, I couldn't help an image of a mum and dad forming around her, the kind of mum and dad she would have – she, small, brave, out of parents smaller, more timid; a father huddled away in his own private world, perhaps; a mum, loving but a bit bewildered with life. A kind of shadow of the parents was there just in thinking of her, as I began writing.

Writing

I must look a strange sight when working on a play. I'm continually jumping up out of my chair, pounding round the room, pulling faces, muttering, then rushing back to my chair again, scribbling a line – then up again. A play is mostly words, of course – I mean, that's what is down in front of you on the page when you read – but words, and the actions, are only the top dressing. Underneath, in the subsoil, are the emotions, the feelings forcing out the words, and the shynesses and the fears that restrict the words and sometimes stop them entirely. All the characters are reacting to each other, responding, fighting their own fight to keep their end up, and hastily, as an end product – a kind of mixture of offensive or defensive weapons – poking their words (and actions) out at each other. Even the love-making is a sort of battle, in a way – a battle with loving weapons, a kind of contest in giving.

Well, that is what happens in real life, or doesn't it? And that is what has to be happening in a play. The only trouble is, of course, that all my characters are not doing their own independent thing. They're all battling away inside *me*. So I am flinging myself into each in turn – and it *is* a kind of flinging, a physical exploding into each, trying to feel how they feel, how they're reacting, and out of that comes a few strangled words, or a flood of words, and I rush to my paper, write it down, look at it, cross it out perhaps, try again, then write again . . . . Yes, it's exhausting. And anyone looking on would think I was quite mad (my family have learned to ignore it). In the midst of all this, I have to take note of another character inside my head – myself. I have to be looking for where each scene can end, and where it is going, and is it all making sense – and how is time passing, because this initial interest of the boy in the girl, and vice versa, has to be established quickly.

And "boy" and "girl", that too. I have to worry, at intervals, that I haven't any names for my characters yet. These have to emerge somehow, names that fit, names that can *mean* the characters to me. Half the first scenes are written with just vague capital letters marking out who is speaking, until, over meals, breaks for cups of tea, I begin to find what to call these damn people. Berenice, yes, that will do for the snobbish mother. Russell, the father (I pinched that from a fellow teacher's teacher-husband). Liza for the girl, a small, strong name. The boy, Paul – soft, hinting at weakness, and the kind of name the mother might choose; Anne, another. Also now Liza's parents have re-emerged on the scene. The father's occupations? Over another cup of tea, I work that out. Works in the parks, yes. I remember a park keeper I chatted with, disconcerting me – hoping for gardening hints – with his complete lack of interest in matters horticultural. So the dad becomes that park keeper, as well as the small private figure huddled away in his . . . And so it goes on, and the first scenes get written, and rewritten, until I'm more or less satisfied with them and, hopefully, they read so naturally that nobody will think anyone slaved over them at all.

Small problems, and solutions

At this point, as I pushed on with the love affair, Paul calling on Liza, I had another phone conversation with Andrée. Most of the play was to be recorded in a studio, but she wanted, for various good reasons, to include about ten minutes of location shooting. Again for good reasons (economy!), this location shooting had to involve only the two lovers. We discussed possible locations. I suggested a Youth Hostel I had recently stayed in, and the parks in London were another obvious possibility. I had begun thinking that the play should not end just at the pregnancy and the probable break-up of the affair (because I could feel that with the characters I had – Paul's parents, Paul – a break-up was due to happen). I wanted to write a kind of epilogue, a re-meeting of the two lovers to show them a few years on, the affair behind them, how it perhaps had changed them both. This would fit neatly into a location scene, probably a good six or seven minutes worth. This was soon agreed, and our conversation could have ended quite happily there. However, Andrée finished up with one final query; what were we going to call the play, by the way?

I dislike thinking up titles. It's a pain. But titles matter. Something apt, relevant . . . . I can waste days trying to come up with something suitable. I put the problem away in the back of my mind and carried on writing. Yet almost immediately – and for the first time in my life without any real effort – I found a title. It seemed to fit. Consequences of a love affair, consequences of parents being out of touch with their children, and – now I had the final scene – consequences of breaking up the affair and running out on your girl. So that was the title out of the way, thank God. You can see, too, the story of the play was more or less set now. I was not yet sure of all the details, but the characters were dictating nicely the way to go. You have to follow your characters. Once you start with a good situation, full of possibilities of conflict, and you have the right sort of characters, then really all you have to do is follow them in and out of the battles and you should have a good script – or, at least, a watchable one – at the finish. You can't afford to play tricks with your characters, forcing them to do things against their nature. If you do, you'll lose your audience – they will stop believing in them. Sometimes time or necessity seems to force you to push some of your minor characters around a little – I did that in this play with Anne, the sister, and the result is she is maybe a bit sentimental, silly – but you *have* to play fair with your main characters.

So I was following my characters, the writing was coming easily, I was finding the openings for location scenes and I even had my title. Within a week or so, the first half was complete.

Reading, and more writing

I took it off to Andrée to read it to her. It's not usual, probably, for authors to give recitals of their plays to directors – certainly not the highly dramatic ones I indulge in – but I prefer to. I know how each scene should go, with what pace, what emotions, and so can give the director perhaps a better idea of the intended effect than can be got from just reading it cold on the page. Also it may help when the director finally gets to grips with the actors. There is a limit to the directions you can put down in the actual writing – "angrily", "more angrily", "eyes blazing", "frothing at the mouth", and so on. Actors don't like too much of that sort of thing. It gets in the way of their own creativity, ties them down too much. They must be allowed some freedom to do their own "flinging" of themselves into the characters.

Andrée liked the reading (the play, I mean, not my performance – she was nice enough not to comment on *that*). But she was slightly worried there was too much comedy, not enough of the serious side of the story. I reassured her that was all in train for the second half (which was true enough). So I got back to my writing. Again it came easily. I was enjoying myself. I felt at ease with the characters, feeling I was discovering more about them as I progressed – the father, Liza, Paul. At times I felt as if I were almost writing in a dream, that I didn't have to strive, flinging myself in and out of the characters – their words came without much conscious effort. So in the end the second half was written, and rewritten, even more quickly than the first.

I gave another reading for Andrée. She had no criticisms this time – apart from some worry that the whole play might now over-run its sixty minutes. I went back, did some cutting – a painful process, but probably beneficial (most plays are overwritten, the characters talk too much). I then typed everything out more or less neatly, changing and rewriting a few things as I went, and posted it all off.

Final reflections

I suppose this ends the story as far as the writing is concerned. But, of course, I was still very much involved – phone calls to discuss casting, more discussions about the script. The location shooting was scheduled to take place before the main rehearsals began, with a couple of days rehearsal and three days filming. Andrée invited me to Ealing Studios to view the rushes. I sat with Andrée and Peter Evans, the film editor, running the film onto a small projection machine, arguing the merits of each take. It was my first view of the lovers, of course. Exciting, and yet a little frightening. How would the scenes go? Would they play as well as I hoped they would?

It was an interesting experience. The first park scene, where Paul babbles about the trees and the flowers, was played much more slowly than I had imagined it – yet it still seemed to work! Then in the last scene, Daniel Abineri as Paul broke down into tears. This again was a surprise. But Paul obviously felt it that way. Andrée had reshot the scene, minus the tears, and viewing both takes it was obvious which was the better. So the tears stayed in, and the scene looked fine. And Sylvestra le Touzel seemed perfect as Liza. I went home happy.

Came the main rehearsals. I attended the first read-through. The script still seemed a little too long. So more cuts. Then, ten days later, the "author's" run-through, the day before the play goes into the studio. A final timing now showed the play was *under* running. So some cuts hastily re-instated. I then sat through one long day in the director's control box watching the recording of the first part, and fidgeted and worried so much that I was excused attendance for the second part.

And that really is the end – except perhaps for one last memory. After the press showing a month or so later, a lady from the Daily Mail approached Andrée's secretary. Oh, yes, it was very good, but isn't it . . well . . too *adult* for school audiences? I enjoyed that. *Consequences* was intended to be adult. School audiences deserve adult plays.

Coins Against the Wall

David Hopkins

The Cast

Harry Briars
Katherine Briars, *his wife*
David Briars, *their fourteen-year-old son*
Arthur
Mick
Jimmy
Singet Rey
— *schoolboys, the same age as David*
Teacher
Mr Matthews, *the headmaster*
Schoolchildren

Coins Against the Wall

1 The Briars's house: living/dining room

Katherine and Harry Briars are eating breakfast. Their son David is sitting quietly with them. Katherine is a somewhat cloying, over-protective woman who tends to fuss over home, husband and son. Harry wishes – and by now he's virtually given up on the idea – that his son was more like him, or more like a son should be. David is shy and intense, a boy who finds it difficult to relate to his school-fellows. They are obviously in the middle of a discussion. Harry is somewhat exasperated; Katherine, concerned and worried. David, unhappy, is wishing he wasn't there.

HARRY I'm not saying it matters. Am I saying it matters?

David shrugs his shoulders.

HARRY I'm just saying try harder.
KATHERINE (*shaking her head*) Harry!
HARRY What do you mean – "Harry"? Harry!
KATHERINE You keep on at him.
HARRY He needs getting on at. Sometimes.

Harry isn't angry, or shouting. He is just repeating things that he's obviously said before.

HARRY Look – what I'm saying is that if he was a bit more like other lads . . . tried a bit, you know, to do better, I don't know. Look, I'm not a teacher, but, Katherine, he doesn't do *anything*.
KATHERINE Yes he does. He . . .
HARRY Just moons about. Won't get anywhere, mooning about.

There is a pause.

HARRY Yes, even now – look at him – sitting there, not saying anything.

KATHERINE He doesn't have to talk all the time.

HARRY Should have something to say for himself.

KATHERINE Boys are different, Harry. Some want one thing, some another.

HARRY Don't you think I know that?

KATHERINE Well!

HARRY You talk to me as if I'm a moron. I know that.

KATHERINE David thinks a lot. (*To David*) Don't you?

HARRY Sitting around dreaming. Mooning about all over the place. He's got no hobbies. He doesn't read books, doesn't read the paper. No friends. Is that my son? (*A bit ashamed*). All I'm saying is that he should get up and do something. (*Finishing his cup of tea*) That's all I'm saying.

He quickly pecks Katherine on the cheek and looks at David who is sitting, head bowed. Harry purses his lips, shakes his head and exits.

KATHERINE See you tonight dear.

HARRY Yes.

The front door bangs closed. Katherine looks at David, wanting to say something.

KATHERINE More tea...?

David shakes his head.

KATHERINE It'll do you good.

She pours him another cup.

KATHERINE You could you know, David,...

David looks up at her.

KATHERINE For your father's sake...

David frowns questioningly.

KATHERINE Try harder.

DAVID Oh, Mum...

KATHERINE Now...now...

She quickly strokes his hair. He pushes her hand away impatiently.

KATHERINE All right. (*She sits and drinks her tea*) I know it might seem silly to you, but couldn't you try to be...?

DAVID I'm no good at sport, Mum; I wish I was, but...

KATHERINE Do more things, you know, not just games. Your father would like you to be . . .

DAVID Bigger and tougher, I know.

KATHERINE All I'm doing is trying to explain to you why, sometimes, your father might seem to . . .

DAVID (*suddenly*) Can I have 50p (*pause*) Please.

KATHERINE Again?

DAVID It's to save towards the school outing – I told you.

KATHERINE It was only the other day you wanted money for . . .

DAVID If you don't want to, just say so.

KATHERINE Of course, David. All right, eh? All right.

2 School playground

It's morning break. Children from about thirteen upwards are milling around the area. In one corner, and seemingly isolated, as well as away from supervision, are three boys – David, Arthur and Mick. It is important that money games cannot be seen by staff on playground duty. Mick keeps watch. Arthur is large and fleshy and the same age as David. He smiles easily and quickly and obviously dominates not only this little group but the classroom as well. Mick is smaller and slighter and seems to be an acolyte of Arthur. They are playing "Coins Against the Wall" This is played by each boy, in turn, throwing a coin towards a wall some six feet away. The player whose coin lands closest to the wall wins and takes the other boys' money. Arthur throws his coin; it bounces against the wall and falls back about six inches.

ARTHUR Not so good . . . but perhaps good enough.

Mick throws his and it falls further away. David takes his time, holding his coin carefully.

ARTHUR New technique this time, eh?

David smiles nervously. He lobs the coin towards the wall. It bounces back further than the others.

ARTHUR Bad luck, David, my son.

Arthur picks up the coins.
A little way off two boys – Jimmy and Singet Rey – both about David's age, are leaning against a wall watching the game.

ARTHUR You go first this time, Mick.

They go through the same ritual. This time it appears that David's is fractionally closer. He starts to smile.

MICK Arthur's nearest.
DAVID I thought mine was.
MICK (*picking up coins*) As an unbiased judge . . .
ARTHUR (*smiling*) Yes, Dave?

Pause

ARTHUR Were you going to say something?

David looks at him.

ARTHUR About who's won? Going to say something about that were you? Right.

He holds out his hand. Mick gives him the money.

ARTHUR David, my old mate – away you go.

David shakes his head.

ARTHUR It's you to go.

Pause. Arthur flicks David's lapels lightly.

ARTHUR Come on, my son.
DAVID Haven't got any more money.
ARTHUR You haven't got what?
DAVID Lost it all.
ARTHUR Already? Now, you can't have, David . . .

We cut again to Jimmy and Singet Rey who see what's going on and turn away casually. To any not close to, it seems a friendly game. It's only Arthur's manner of speech and small physical movements, together with David's fear gives it away.

ARTHUR Ah well – better luck next time.
MICK Yes – get a bit of practice in.

The bell rings for the end of break.

ARTHUR There you are – couldn't have gone on anyway.
MICK No.
ARTHUR Ran out at just the right time, didn't you?

David smiles again and nods.

ARTHUR See you tomorrow then.

DAVID I don't think I can . . .

ARTHUR Same time, same place, as my old lady often says.

MICK As per usual.

ARTHUR Eh?

MICK That's what my old lady says.

ARTHUR Oh. (*To David*) What does your old lady say?

David shrugs.

ARTHUR Give him the money?

MICK (*laughing*) Yes.

ARTHUR Bet that's what she says.

He smiles at David – a broad genuine smile.

ARTHUR So, tomorrow, David, OK? You'll have some more money. (*touching David's chin very lightly*) Won't you?

MICK Course he will.

ARTHUR Course he will. Just asks his old lady, that's all he's got to do. (*Smiling broadly.*) Right Dave?

David looks around but all the other pupils are strolling back to the classrooms, except Jimmy and Singet who are looking in his direction. David looks appealingly toward them but the two lads just move on sheepishly.

3 The classroom

David is staring – frowning and worried – out of the window while the teacher begins the lesson.

TEACHER What we have to remember is that the sun is considerably closer than the other stars; that's why it appears to be larger. In fact it is quite a small and insignificant star when compared with the myriads of other bodies in the universe. Nonetheless, without it, our planet would cease to exist. Without what, David?

There's a pause.

TEACHER David Briars?

David looks at him quickly, completely unaware of what's been said.

TEACHER Stand up and tell the class – and me – what would happen to our planet without what? Stand up David.

David stands. He looks around, perplexed and unsure. The one face he sees, grinning at him is that of Arthur.

4 The classroom

Afternoon. We can hear the sound of children playing. David and his form teacher are alone in the room. David is sheepish and unsure, the same attitude as we saw with his father.

TEACHER I know it's a bit of a nerve asking you to stay in during break – specially the short afternoon break but, well, I feel it's time we had a bit of a talk, don't you?

Pause

TEACHER Anything you want to talk to me about, David?

David shakes his head.

TEACHER You look fed up to me, David. What's wrong? Trouble at home?

David shakes his head.

TEACHER Trouble with your mates?
DAVID (*quietly*) No, sir.

Pause. The teacher sees there is nothing more to be said. David looks at him.

TEACHER (*smiling*) Well if there is ever anything you want to talk about, you can always talk to me.
DAVID Okay, sir.
TEACHER Leave it up to you, then, right? Anything you want to discuss, just come and see me, eh?

5 Bus-stop

A group of school children are waiting for the bus to take them home. In the middle, in a little group, are David, Jimmy and Singet Rey.

JIMMY Bus is late.
REY Bus's always late.
JIMMY Yes, then there's all those kids from Hannington packing in already.
REY Yea.
JIMMY (*edgy*) Where's your mates, Dave?

DAVID What?
JIMMY Arthur and Mick. Spending a lot of time with them.
REY Don't knock around with us so much do you?
DAVID It's not that.
JIMMY You mustn't half like playing that game.
REY Do you? Do you really like playing it?
JIMMY Seems boring to me.
DAVID Jimmy, I...
JIMMY What?
DAVID It's... it's that game with Arthur and Mick, it's not really...
REY Here's the bus.
JIMMY Come on! Quick!
DAVID Jimmy, I don't know what to do. I...

But they're not listening.

6 The Briars's house

It is morning. David is standing in the centre of the room, frowning. He is obviously very unhappy and unsure. We – but David doesn't – see Katherine standing in the doorway looking at him. She is frowning, irritated and upset. David is suddenly aware of her. His head jerks up and he looks at her.

DAVID Mum...
KATHERINE 'Bout time you were off to school. You'll be late if you don't hurry.

She starts tidying his hair and collar. Even though David – as we have seen – dislikes this, he does nothing to prevent her.

DAVID Mum...
KATHERINE David, some of the other mothers – now I wasn't checking up on you – but, well, I was talking to some of the other mothers, and they said their children aren't saving for an outing. Now, I don't mind if you want to buy extra things, but, David...
DAVID Mum, please...
KATHERINE I feel awful. You've been getting money out of me for I don't know what.
DAVID It's important.
KATHERINE Lying to me.
DAVID No...
KATHERINE You're not getting this money to save for an outing though.

(*Pause*) David. (*Pause*) We've always taught you to tell the truth. If I was to tell your father.

David looks at her suddenly.

KATHERINE I won't. Of course. But David . . .!

She relents and quickly kisses him. David reacts slightly against it.

DAVID Mum, if I don't . . .

KATHERINE You'll be late for school. Come on now. That'd never do.

7 The classroom

The teacher is preparing the first class; he is drawing a diagram on the blackboard. Behind him we hear and see the low hubbub of the kids as they slowly settle down. We look at David as he sits quietly by himself. He sees Arthur across the classroom. Arthur smiles and, if you didn't know, you'd say it was a genuinely friendly greeting. He nudges Mick who looks up and also gives a broad friendly grin at David. The teacher turns around.

TEACHER Right then, you lot – settle down.

8 The playground

ARTHUR You'll just have to, won't you, David?

MICK You know how much we like our game.

ARTHUR Very disappointed . . .

MICK We'll be . . .,

ARTHUR . . . if we miss it. Right, my son?

DAVID I can't ask my mother for . . .

ARTHUR (*grinning*) Oh, but you can.

He is slowly, and threateningly, stroking the side of David's chin.

ARTHUR Of course you can.

David's knees buckle, the reason being that Mick has pushed his own knee into the back of David's. David is looking thoroughly frightened.

ARTHUR Right, Mick?

MICK Oh I'm sure.

ARTHUR Your mother dotes on you. Do anything for you.

MICK Not like us.

ARTHUR No, we're different.

MICK Deprived of parental affection, us.

In another corner of the playground Jimmy and Singet Rey are again watching – this time they can see that David isn't happy with what's going on.

REY Do you think we should . . .?
JIMMY No, let Dave sort it out. None of our business, Singy.
REY No.

With one last look in David's direction, they move off.

ARTHUR Don't look so worried, Briars.
MICK Nothing to be worried about.
ARTHUR Just want to continue with our game that's all.
MICK That's right.
ARTHUR You enjoy it don't you?
MICK Our game?
ARTHUR Of course he does. See you tomorrow, David.

9 The Briars's house

Evening. The family are watching television, Katherine and Harry sitting in their respective armchairs, and David at the table. A football match is in progress; Harry is watching it excitedly, while David is not really watching at all.

HARRY (*reacting to the game*) Come on Ref! David, did you see that? (*pause*) Not again! They haven't come to play football, that lot. (*Turning to David*) Eh?

David, feigning interest, nods. Unhappily he looks from his father's agitated face to his mother, placidly eating chocolates as she reads a paperback. He bites his lip, stands and quietly exits. A goal is scored, and the crowd's reaction reaches a crescendo. Harry gleefully bangs the arm of his chair. Katherine, disinterestedly, glances at the set.

10 The living/dining room

It is early morning. David quietly opens the door and enters. He looks around. He moves to the sideboard and quickly searches on it. He looks on the table and then in the corner of the armchair, finds it: his mother's handbag. He moves and looks down at it. He is obviously unhappy at what he is going to do. The ticking of the clock sounds very loud. He almost has to force himself to reach out and pick up the handbag. He opens it and, now that he's made the decision, quickly rifles through it. He hears something, turns and find his mother – in her dressing-gown – standing there.

KATHERINE You're up early, David.

David can't say anything.

KATHERINE Got something on have you?

She comes into the room. David is frozen.

KATHERINE Are you all right? What's that you've . . .?

She sees the handbag in David's hand. He's made no effort to hide it.

KATHERINE David . . .! Have you been at my handbag? I can't believe . . .

David moves past her towards the door.

KATHERINE Stealing from my . . .

David reaches the door.

KATHERINE David!

He realises that he still has the handbag. He reaches back and puts it quickly on the sideboard and then exits.

KATHERINE Come back here!

She is very upset. She crosses to the sideboard and, irrationally, snaps her handbag shut.

11 The classroom

The form teacher is calling the morning register.

TEACHER Astle.
BOY Sir.
TEACHER Ayers.
BOY Sir.
TEACHER Bernes.
GIRL Sir.
TEACHER Briars.

No answer.

TEACHER Briars.

Arthur and Mick look at each other.

TEACHER Cook.
BOY Sir.

12 Street scene

We cut to watch David strolling aimlessly along through a parade of shops. Finally he sits down forlornly on a bench.

13 The Briars's house

They are eating their evening meal. Harry is preoccupied with his paper. David is toying with his food. Katherine, still very upset by the morning's happenings, looks at David. David looks up, catches her eye for a second, then looks down again.

14 The classroom

Morning register again.

TEACHER Bernes.
GIRL Sir.
TEACHER Briars.

No answer.

TEACHER Briars.

15 The Briars's house

It is evening.

KATHERINE Answer me.

Katherine is hurt and angry, quite unable to control the situation. David, to begin with, is truculent and unhappy.

KATHERINE I won't have you standing there, saying nothing.

Pause.

KATHERINE Where have you been?

Pause.

KATHERINE David!

David shakes his head and makes for the door.

KATHERINE Don't walk out on me.

He stops.

KATHERINE (*trying a softer approach*) Every morning you've been leaving th house – saying "good-bye" – every evening you've been tellin me about your day at school and – David – you haven't bee going for over a week. Maybe that's what you should be whe you leave school – an actor. You fooled me.

David doesn't react. Katherine moves towards him.

KATHERINE Will you tell me? I want to help.

David still doesn't react. The anger is growing in Katherine again.

KATHERINE Can you imagine how I felt? Your teacher knocked on tha door – my door – asking how you were. Why weren't you a school, he was asking. Put yourself in my place. (*Taking him b the shoulders*) It's no good just standing there saying nothing. won't have it. Where have you been?

DAVID (*shaking his head*) Nowhere.

KATHERINE Nowhere! A boy of mine – playing truant. Can you imagin how I feel? What's happened to you? I've always boaste about you – what a good boy you are. I know your father wishe you were a bit more . . . but to me . . .? David, I don't under stand what's happening to you. Lying, stealing, playin truant. Now you're my son, David. I want to know.

David looks at her, quickly and angrily. He then shakes her hand off an moves away.

KATHERINE Don't walk away from me.

DAVID I'm not walking away from you.

KATHERINE Can't you understand how humiliated I felt? Can't you se that?

DAVID (*swinging back to face her*) Is that all you care about? You feelin humiliated.

KATHERINE Don't shout at me! (*Quietly*) What's the matter? Tell me – I'r your mother. I want to help you, David!

DAVID I keep losing.

KATHERINE Losing?

DAVID I play this game – and I keep losing.

KATHERINE What game? David?

DAVID (*shrugging*) A game.

KATHERINE (*slowly realising*) A game for money? David – you shouldn't play games for money. (*Suddenly*) Is that why you were...! David, you shouldn't.

She takes his face in her hands.

KATHERINE Why do you go on playing? You don't have to go on playing.

He pulls away from her.

KATHERINE David.

David slowly sinks into a chair, head turned away in embarrassment. Katherine immediately sits beside him and puts her arms around him.

KATHERINE What is it? David...

She strokes his hair.

KATHERINE There, Come on. Tell me. There.

DAVID (*very quietly*) It's those lads. They keep making me bring them money.

KATHERINE *Make* you? Why didn't you tell me? Is that why you needed the money? Oh, David. (*Rocking him gently*) I know we shouldn't have sent you to that school. We should have found you one in a better neighbourhood and...

David breaks away and stands.

KATHERINE Why didn't you...?

DAVID Don't tell Dad.

KATHERINE Not if...

DAVID Please don't tell Dad.

KATHERINE No.

DAVID You mustn't. Look, can't you and I sort it out? Just you and me.

KATHERINE Your father could deal with it better.

DAVID Can't I just go to another school? Just take me away from it and... can't I?

KATHERINE Of course you can. Of course you can.

She hugs him again.

DAVID Don't tell Dad.

KATHERINE Anything you want. My David.

16 The Briars's dining room

David is not really eating. Katherine is slurping back cups of tea. Harry is eating his breakfast with determination. Silence. All three deep in their own thoughts. Suddenly…

HARRY What's this your mother tells me?

David looks at him quickly. Then turns to look at Katherine. She can't meet his gaze.

HARRY Eh? Eh? I mean what did they say? Bring us some money or we'll pull your hair?

David laughs quickly and nervously. There is a pause.

HARRY My son! (*Suddenly, to Katherine*) This is all your fault. That's what I think. What am I supposed to do? Take him by the hand, go down to the school with him and say, "My lad is being bullied?" I mean, how do you think I'll feel?

DAVID Mum. I asked you not to…

KATHERINE He's your father. He cares what…

HARRY This is what comes of tying him to your apron-strings.

KATHERINE I just wanted him to be…

HARRY Goodness knows what you wanted him to be. Sometimes I think you wanted him to be a blessed girl. Well, I'm beginning to think you've got one. Don't you think a normal boy would sometimes, just sometimes want to go to a football match with his father, *want* to go to boxing lessons when his father offers to pay, want to try to learn to look after himself? (*To David*) What did you say when I offered to pay for lessons? Do you remember? "Please, Mum! Please, Mum!" So he didn't go.

There is a long silence. Harry knows he has gone too far. David is nearly crying.

HARRY (*quieter*) I'm not going to that school with him.

KATHERINE You don't have to.

HARRY (*to David*) No more money, no more games, no more crying, no more sulks. You can go to that school tomorrow. You face up to them and try standing up for yourself, just once in your life. I can tell you one thing. I bet that lad who's been taking your mother's money off you – right or wrong – I bet you his Dad's not ashamed of him.

Katherine's lips firm up with resolution.

17 Headmaster's study

David is standing in front of the desk. Mr Matthews, the Headmaster, is a man in his late thirties, dresses casually, but not too casually. He has modern ideas, but not too modern; he believes that education should be child-centred, but not too child-centred. He believes that he is liked and respected by the pupils. His attitude as we come into the scene is somehow as if David is in some sort of trouble. We would certainly feel, if we'd not seen the earlier scenes, that David has been summoned to be taken to task and made to apologise for a misdemeanour.

MATTHEWS There's no real excuse, you know. I mean, staying away from school for a whole week, there's no excuse. Playing truant – that's what it amounts to, doesn't it, David? Isn't it strange that we say *playing* truant about something so serious? With your exams coming up, you know, that week of *playing* truant might affect your whole life. Quite apart from that, David, I have legal obligations to see that you come to school and that you're educated – until you're sixteen. You know that, don't you?

DAVID Sir.

MATTHEWS Are you bored with school, David?

DAVID No, sir.

MATTHEWS Good. School used to be like medicine: it did you good, so it didn't matter if you didn't like the taste. But now a teacher wants to see boys and girls happy, relaxed, learning and getting ready for life, you know. I'd sooner you got ready for life here – not hanging round the streets.

DAVID Sir.

MATTHEWS And so would your mother. She was very distressed when she came to see me. Some mothers might not care too much, but your mother most certainly does. So I had to assure her, and I'll assure you too, that I'm a caring Headmaster and I have a caring staff. Would you agree, David?

DAVID Yes, sir.

MATTHEWS Then why did you not come and see me or your form master? It's sometimes very hard to talk to people who are nearest to you, your parents. But I'm very disappointed that you found it hard to talk to me or your form master. We both have families of our own, you know. Did you think I'd be surprised, David, at what was going on? Do you think it would have been news to me?

Pause. David is a bit surprised.

MATTHEWS Every school has its Arthurs and its Micks. I'm well aware of the sort of boys those are. Any teacher sees plenty of bully boys – and girls – and I've seen how many of them end up in later life. I knew one day those lads would go too far. Do you know what extortion means, David?

DAVID Yes, sir.

MATTHEWS Well, I think we'd both agree that extortion is going too far, wouldn't we?

18 The classroom

Mick, Arthur, David and the Headmaster are standing in front of the class.

MATTHEWS There are different sorts of bullying. I'd imagine that the one we think of first is physical – physical. The victim being violently set upon. But there are others. Supposing I looked up "bullying" in the dictionary – what would I find?

The class is in no mood to answer.

MATTHEWS "Bullying: to persecute, oppress, tease, physically or morally." We're fortunate to live in a country which is not run by bullies or tyrants. Others aren't so lucky and I don't think you'd want to change places with them. And I doubt very much if any of you want to be called a bully, either – because bully isn't the same as tough or strong – bullies are blusterers, cowards, tyrants. Do you like to be called a bully, Arthur?

ARTHUR No, sir.

MATTHEW Michael?

MICK No, sir.

MATTHEWS I'm darned sure you don't. But you were exactly that – bullies, tyrants! – cowards? Cowards, Arthur?

ARTHUR No, sir.

MATTHEW Cowards, Michael?

MICK No, sir.

MATTHEWS Go back to your desk.

David hasn't moved.

MATTHEWS David.

David slowly returns to his desk. There is silence as the Headmaster leaves and the door closes. Silence is maintained for two seconds.

19 The playground

David is alone. Friends pass him by; Arthur and Mick stand with their gang.

MATTHEWS (*voice over*) Suppose I looked up "bullying" in a dictionary. What would I find?

We watch the lonely figure of David.

The Kids are Okay

Jack Ronder

The Cast

Kenny, *fifteen years old*
Jill, *his thirteen-year-old sister*
Andrew, *their father*
Mary, *their mother*
Mr Mulveen, *teacher*
Car driver
Doreen, *Andrew's girl-friend*
Gran, *Mary's mother*
Barman

The Kids are Okay

Part One: *Who's leaving?*

1 A classroom

Set in a comprehensive school in Glasgow. A close-up of Kenny Smith in the front row of a maths class, with other boys and girls at their desks. Kenny is a tall, ginger, lanky fifteen-year-old. He is leaning his head against his hand, fed up and far away. Mr Mulveen, the teacher, comes up to Kenny's desk.

MULVEEN What's the matter, Kenny? Where's the brains gone? Teacher's speaking.

Kenny looks up.

MULVEEN (*sarcastic*) A nice face. (*pause*) Where's your homework?

Kenny shrugs.

MULVEEN I didn't catch your answer, Kenny. Where's your homework?
KENNY I haven't done it.
MULVEEN And why is that?

Kenny shrugs.

MULVEEN Say again?
KENNY I don't know.
MULVEEN Too hard?
KENNY I don't know.
MULVEEN Is there anything wrong?
KENNY No.
MULVEEN (*sharply*) I want that homework by tomorrow. Do you understand?
KENNY Yes.

The bell goes for the end of school.

2 A council estate

Groups of grey, two-storey housing blocks with gardens. Jill, walking home alone, is approaching her own gate. Kenny and a friend are on bikes. The friend waves and turns off; Kenny cycles to his gate as Jill is opening it.

JILL Hi.
KENNY 'Lo.

Kenny dismounts as he goes through the gate. Jill shuts it after them. Kenny leans his bike against the house-wall, padlocks it and takes his gear from the carrier. We see the garden is uncared-for. Kenny and Jill arrive at the main door together, Jill fishing for her keys in her purse. Jill inserts the key in the lock, turns it and opens the door. They go in, Kenny shutting the door after them.

3 The hall

Jill sees some overalls in a heap on the stairs.

JILL Dad's home.
KENNY (*seeing Mum's coat*) So's Mum.

He is about to enter the living room when he hears their parents arguing.

ANDREW (*voice only*) Let's leave it! We're not gonna get anywhere with this.
MARY (*voice only*) Well – I need a holiday – and I'll go on my own then.
ANDREW You go! I'm not stopping you.
MARY Andy, put that paper down. You're not going to sink in there and go to sleep! You're not ducking out of it like that!
ANDREW I'll do what I bloody well like! Jeez. Go on, go and gawp at Pedro on the Costa Brava. Do what you want woman – just give us peace.
MARY And you'll do what you want, is it?
ANDREW I'm me, I'm no changing. I'm no going to gargle with your Spanish bloody wine . . .

Kenny pushes open the door to the living-room.

4 The living-room

The room has a three-piece suite, a dresser, table and chairs and carpet bought on hire purchase sixteen years ago. They look their age. A

Raeburn fire (unlit) with clock and photos on the mantelpiece – school photos of Kenny and Jill, and holiday photos of Andrew and Mary, much younger, on holiday in Spain. A black and white telly. The cooker and sink are in a small scullery off.

Andrew is sprawled in one of the armchairs by the unlit fire, concentrating on his daily paper. He is forty, a big-built man, but not fat – sandy hair, usually easy-going, a painter by trade, employed full-time on factory maintenance.

Mary is thirty-six, red-haired, buxom, a live wire. She goes hurriedly into the scullery where she noisily fills the kettle as Kenny and Jill come in. She bangs the lid on and puts it on the gas. A silence. Neither Andrew or Mary acknowledge the kids. Kenny drops his bag on the floor, takes off his blazer, puts it on the back of a chair. Jill puts her books on the table and sits.

JILL You're home early.

This is addressed to Andrew. He doesn't react.

MARY (*from the scullery, her back to the kids*) I got the afternoon off.

Jill and Kenny look at her. Kenny turns to his Dad.

KENNY You been fired?

ANDREW No, I haven't been fired! I *took* the afternoon off!

Mary comes through and bangs open the breadbin and bangs it shut again. She opens the cupboard, brings out a biscuit tin and bangs it on the table. She stands there.

MARY D'you want tea, Jill?

JILL Yes please.

MARY Kenny?

Kenny silently nods. Mary goes back to the scullery. Andrew puts his paper down, and appears to think.

ANDREW I wouldna mind a cup.

5 The living-room

It is late evening, a Western is on the television. Kenny and Jill sit at the table with notebooks open, but they are watching the set. Andrew is dozing in his armchair. Mary is clattering around the scullery. She finishes and stands in the doorway.

MARY Thanks for washing up.

The only response is that Jill guiltily drops her eyes from the screen to her notebook.

MARY (*pointed*) Thanks for supper, Mum!

Again, no response. Then Kenny gives her a look.

KENNY (*ironic*) Thanks.

Pause. Mary goes to the set and switches it off. Kenny is more hurt than annoyed.

MARY Do you have to be like him?

Andrew keeps his eyes shut. Mary is furious.

MARY I'm cheesed! . . . I've had enough . . . .!

She goes out muttering.

MARY What the hell's life about . . .?

Her bedroom door is heard slamming. Andrew opens his eyes. He eases himself up from the chair, stands and stretches.

ANDREW I'm going out.
KENNY For a pint?
ANDREW (*hurt and angry too. He advances on Kenny*) Would that be okay son?
KENNY Sorry.
ANDREW (*going out*) Just for peace. That's all . . .

The outside door is heard shutting. Jill twists her hair around. Kenny gets up and switches the set on again.

6 Jill's bedroom

A tiny room with an old iron bedstead and chest of drawers. A square of rug on worn lino, walls and door plastered with pop stars and pages from Jackie. On the chest of drawers and the mantelpiece is a line-up of cheap toy animals, dolls and cut outs.
Jill is in pyjamas, sitting cross-legged on the bed. Her mother can be heard weeping in the next room. Jill looks up, startled, afraid. She comes to a decision, gets up and goes out. The bathroom door is unlocked and Kenny comes out, fully dressed, and crosses to his room.

JILL Kenny –
KENNY What?

Jill nods to Mary's room. Kenny listens.

KENNY So?
JILL Shouldn't we go in?
KENNY I'm not going in.

He goes to his own room and shuts the door. The weeping has subsided. Jill, desolate, twists her hair. She goes to Kenny's door and opens it.

7 Kenny's room

Not much bigger than Jill's, it has a ricketty wooden bed and chest of drawers. Dirty clothes are everywhere. Football teams and newspaper reports cover the walls. Kenny lies back on his bed, staring at the ceiling.

JILL (*from the door*) Kenny?

Kenny doesn't look or answer. Jill comes in, shuts the door, and leans on it.

KENNY What?
JILL What's going to happen?
KENNY What d'you mean?
JILL To them.
KENNY Nothing.
JILL To you and me.
KENNY We're okay.
JILL I don't feel okay.

She comes and sits on the floor opposite him.

JILL Why do they keep having rows?
KENNY I don't know.
JILL They row about us.
KENNY (*shrugging*) They row about everything.
JILL Why?
KENNY Just the way of it.
JILL What can we do?
KENNY (*looks at her in surprise*) Nothing.
JILL Do you know Sharon Ainslie in my class?
KENNY No.
JILL You do! Her Mum and Dad have split.
KENNY So? Half my class has split.
JILL Half?
KENNY Well, some . . . They never had a father.

JILL We do.
KENNY (*uneasy*) They're not going to split.
JILL Where would we go?
KENNY We'd stay here.
JILL Would we? (*Then she blurts out, near to tears*) I don't want Dad to go! (*She subsides and looks around*) You're in a mess here.
KENNY There's nothing clean to wear. No shirts. Mum's not bothering.
JILL I run mine through myself.
KENNY Will you do me a shirt for tomorrow?
JILL No! (*pause*) Which one?
KENNY (*getting up and pulling his dirty clothes around*) Here.
JILL I'm not doing your socks and pants!

She takes the shirt and holds it away from her. She gets up.

JILL If it isn't dry in the morning, too bad. I'm not ironing it.
KENNY Thanks.
JILL Goodnight.
KENNY 'Night.

8 The living-room

Mary switches on the light and enters in her dressing-gown, to take her teacup to the sink. She washes it out and leaves it to drain. She comes back into the living-room, and studies Kenny's pile of school-books on the table. Her eye is caught by something on the floor under the hot water tank. She picks it up. It is Kenny's wet shirt on a wire hanger that has slipped from the tank. She feels it, takes it back to the scullery, rinses the shirt-tails and the cuffs, squeezes dry, and hangs it on the cord above the sink. She comes back out of the living-room and sees the line of light under Kenny's door. She pauses.

MARY Kenny?

She opens the bedroom door.

9 Kenny's bedroom

Kenny is still dressed, sitting on his bed on the pillow with his back to the wall. He has been tearing pages from a notebook and making them into paper darts. The floor is littered with them on top of the other clutter. He throws one as Mary opens the door. She watches it, taking in the mess.

MARY Who washed your shirt?
KENNY Jill.
MARY It was nice of her. She'd hung it on the hot tank and it fell off. I've seen to it.
KENNY Will it be dry?
MARY I'll iron it in the morning. (*Pause*) I see your books are still on the table. You not done your homework?
KENNY No.
MARY Why?
KENNY Not in the mood.
MARY Your Dad's beyond living with.

Kenny keeps his head down.

MARY I wish he'd wake up.

She looks for a response from Kenny, but gets none.

MARY It can't be nice for you. (*She bites her lip at the lack of response*) I'm not clearing this mess. (*Pause*) Goodnight.

Kenny doesn't answer. She shuts the door. Kenny tears another page out, makes a dart, while he hears Mary's voice in the hall outside.

MARY (*voice*) Night Jill, get your light out.
JILL (*voice*) Is Dad not in yet?
MARY (*voice*) No.

10 Jill's room

Jill is in her pyjamas going round all her dolls and animals, touching them, putting them exactly in their place.

JILL (*whispering*) One, one, one, one, one, one, one, one –

She comes to a cut-out scrap fairy stuck to the wall. She touches the wand.

JILL Please . . .

She goes the rounds again.

JILL Two, two, two, two, two, two, two, two –

She again touches the wand.

JILL Please . . . Three, three, three . . .

11 The living-room

It is pitch dark. The key is heard in the outside door, then the sound of the door opening and shutting. The light is switched on. Andrew is there, not drunk. He goes to the settee, sits, and takes off his shoes. He goes out again to the hall, and comes back with an armful of coats to make himself a bed on the settee. Then he realises Mary is standing in the doorway.

MARY Had a good time?
ANDREW No.
MARY The pubs must have shut by now.
ANDREW Ay. I've been walking.
MARY Oh?
ANDREW Just... walking.
MARY Alone?
ANDREW (*flares up*) Ay, woman, alone! What the hell do you think I am!

A pause.

MARY (*thinking aloud*) The kids...
ANDREW Oh ay, the kids. I'm sorry for them.
MARY What d'you mean by that?
ANDREW Shurrup, or they'll hear the lot.
MARY Why sorry for them – because you do nothing for them, is that why?
ANDREW I work for them!
MARY What about some fun for them!
ANDREW Fun? Fun costs money! You think I'm made of it!
MARY Oh money again! Enough for the beer, then home to the telly and sleep, that's it! That's life, is it? Well, I've got mine to live.
ANDREW With who?
MARY What are you saying now?
ANDREW It's surely not with Gran, Gran, the wee society woo-man.
MARY Go on, pick on her!

Andrew and Mary are now in blazing confrontation.

ANDREW Me – pick on her? Tell that to her, the old cow!
MARY She's my mother!
ANDREW But I didna marry her! I don't know how your Dad did!

He starts throwing the coats around.

MARY Are you going to sleep here?

ANDREW If I get any sleep.

MARY Andrew, I'm fed up, fed to the teeth! This bloody house! (*Sobs.*)

ANDREW Who's leaving it then? You? Or me?

He pulls open the door and strides out.

12 The hall

Jill is standing outside her bedroom door, afraid. Andrew subsides and controls his emotions.

ANDREW (*gently*) Go to bed, Jill.

Jill just looks at him.

ANDREW Go on, go to bed.

Jill turns, goes into her room and shuts the door. Andrew takes a breath, goes into his bedroom and comes out with his pyjamas. He returns to sleep in the living-room, his wife just sitting there, her face a mask.

13 The classroom

Mulveen is sitting at his desk flicking over the pages of the textbook.

MULVEEN For tomorrow then, page – eh – ninety-four, the top exercise, do the odd numbers.

The class groans.

MULVEEN Practice, that's all. Kenny Smith, where's your project work?

KENNY Haven't done it.

MULVEEN Why's that?

KENNY Don't know.

MULVEEN I did tell you. (*Pause*) Didn't I?

KENNY Yes.

MULVEEN Could you stand up?

Kenny shambles to his feet.

MULVEEN You'd better come and see me at half past three.

14 The park

Jill is walking along with her school things, looking around. She sees the person she's looking for, and waves. It is her father, sitting on a bench.

ANDREW Hello Jill, come and sit down. Sorry I had to send a message, but I couldn't get you on your own any other way.

JILL Why are you not at the Works?

ANDREW They gave me time off. Where's Kenny?

JILL He's been kept in.

ANDREW Aw Jeez . . . For how long?

JILL I don't know.

ANDREW We'll give him a minute. I need to talk to you.

JILL What about?

ANDREW Well . . . home's not a good place for any of us just now. And I think you and Kenny . . . (*looking round again*) Where is he?

15 The classroom

Kenny is alone at his desk.

MULVEEN Oh, ay. What's the matter with you?

KENNY Don't know.

MULVEEN You're a bright lad, wasting yourself. So what's wrong. Are you in trouble?

KENNY No.

MULVEEN You'll not get on in the big world this way.

Kenny is silent.

MULVEEN I'm trying, Kenny Smith, to tell you something! Why have you stopped working? And I'm speaking as your form master – everybody's saying the same. Sullen, insolent, that's you. Why?

Kenny is silent.

MULVEEN Stand up.

Kenny gets to his feet.

MULVEEN What do you do with yourself?

Kenny gives a big don't-know shrug.

MULVEEN You'll stay in and do the homework. And the project! I think, between you and me, that what you need, my boy, five foot nine or not, is a good shaking. Is your father a big man?

KENNY (*pause*) Yes.

MULVEEN Tell him from me, Kenny Smith, that he'd be doing you a great favour if he just took you by the shoulders, and shook you!

He stalks away to his desk raises the lid and bangs it down.

MULVEEN Sit down and get on with it!

16 The park

Andrew looks at his watch.

ANDREW Did he get my message?

JILL I suppose so.

ANDREW (*worried*) I can't wait. Listen, Jill, I know you were upset last night. I don't want you to be upset. Your Mum and me are... we're having a rough time. Well – marriage is like that. We started off, we fell for each other... it was good. But after a time... it's nothing big, it's just the little things that build up until it... until there's nothing left. You like changing your friends after a time, married people are stuck. It suits some. I hope it suits you when you meet a bloke. But for most of us... well – we shout a bit, and argue a bit. What I'm saying is... not to worry, Jill.

JILL What d'you mean?

ANDREW I mean, you'll be all right, and Kenny'll be all right.

JILL What's going to happen? Are you and Mum...?

ANDREW I don't know, Jill. But I do know that you're mine, and Kenny's mine, and nothing'll ever change that. Have you got that?

JILL Sort of...

ANDREW (*urgently*) Jill, we've had great times, and we will have great times. Here –

He takes a bundle of pound notes from his breast pocket, where he'd put them in readiness, and stuffs them into her hand.

ANDREW Split that between Kenny and you. And just keep quiet at home. For a bit. And do your best. We'll all draw back into the goal. Defend. Peace. We'll keep trying. I promise, we'll keep trying. Tell Kenny.

17 The classroom

Kenny is working in his project book. Mulveen at his desk looks at his watch, gets up and comes over to Kenny.

MULVEEN Great! You can do it! Kenny Smith, this is going to be a good project. Off you go now – finish it at home. We'll show it at the open day.

Kenny exits and walks towards the cycle sheds. He throws his project book over the shed roof, unpadlocks the bike and cycles off. We watch him almost collide with a car as he leaves the school gates . . . the driver mouths furiously – Kenny gives the V-sign before setting off up the road.

18 The living-room

The family are eating their sausage and eggs in silence.

ANDREW Why were you kept in?
KENNY Mathematics.
ANDREW Too hard for you?
KENNY I don't know, I'm not bothered.

Silence again.

MARY School okay?
JILL Ay.

Conscious silence.

MARY Do you need your football gear washed for Saturday?
KENNY Ay.

Silence.

ANDREW (*to Jill*) Okay?
JILL Okay.

She suddenly pushes her chair back, gets up and goes out.

KENNY What a home! I'd be better living in a tent in Ibrox Park! And begging for my food!

He gets up. He wants to say more to his mother and father, but can't, and goes to his bedroom.

19 The council block

Andrew is making his way down the path to the gate. He has his coat on and carries a battered old suitcase, heavily laden. He goes out of sight without looking back.
Kenny and Jill (clutching her animals) have watched this from their bedrooms, while Mary has stood frozen in the hall. She takes a deep breath and goes to Kenny's room.

20 Kenny's room

Kenny turns from the window as Mary switches the light on. He looks straight at her, almost accusingly. She sniffs the air.

MARY Have you been smoking?

Kenny brings a newly lit cigarette from behind his back. He is defiant.

MARY Where'd you get the money?
KENNY Dad.
MARY You're a fool. Put it out.

Kenny looks at the cigarette, opens the curtains wide and flicks it through the open window.

MARY I want to talk to you.

At that moment Jill appears in the doorway, still clasping one of her animals.

MARY C'mere, the pair of you. That was Dad going off.
KENNY For good?
MARY Could be . . . It can't have come as a surprise to you, because we've been having these rows. We decided tonight, there was no use going on, not in the meantime. It's been a long time coming, but it's a shock.
JILL We'll see him?
MARY Oh ay. You will.
KENNY Where's he gone?
MARY He'll be staying at your Uncle Jimmy's till he sees what's what. Listen – he wasn't happy; I wasn't happy; and you can't be happy. I'm not blaming anyone (*almost in tears*).
JILL Will we be put out of the house?
MARY No. (*Pause*) I've got my money coming in from the agency. Dad'll have to send your keep, your clothes. You'll see him. We'll arrange . . . We'll manage. We'll have to. . . .

Part Two: *One year later.*

21 The classroom

Mulveen is behind his desk, with registers. Mary is sitting on the other side.

MULVEEN Kenny's doing not bad, Mrs Smith. He seems to have got down to it.

MARY Good news for a change.

MULVEEN Yes, he's had a rough patch. Maths he'll get, and French and English and he's a fair chance in History. And his practical subjects, so he's well away. I was sorry to hear about your troubles at home, but I take it things have settled.

MARY Yes. We've separated, a year now, so at least there's peace.

MULVEEN Kenny's certainly made up for lost ground. I can't say fairer than that. Would you consider him staying on for his Highers?

MARY Could he get them?

MULVEEN Oh, yes, he could have a fair stab. Let's talk about it nearer the time.

MARY Fine! (*Getting up to go*) How's Jill's work?

MULVEEN (*hesitant*) She's doing okay. She has a couple of years to go, though. Do they see their father?

MARY (*grim*) They do. Once a week. Every Sunday he takes them out. Spoils them to blazes.

22 The council block – street outside

The garden rubbish has been cleared away, the lawn and borders now look cared for. The front door opens and Jill and Kenny come out, dressed in clean, crisp casuals. Jill has a raincoat, Kenny a bomber jacket. Mary comes out with them. She is in blouse and slacks and slippers.

MARY Is he there?

Jill looks around to see Andrew in an open-necked shirt and necktie, leaning against a garden wall some way along the street.

JILL He's waiting.

MARY Bye then.

JILL Bye Mum.

KENNY Bye.

Kenny and Jill walk along, then cross the road to Andrew.

ANDREW Hi, kiddies!
KENNY (*smiling*) Hello, Dad.
JILL Hello, Dad.
ANDREW Come and see.

He crosses the road again with them, to where a gleaming clean Escort is parked.

ANDREW How's that then?
KENNY Hey, have you hired it?
ANDREW (*brightly*) Ask no questions. Get in.
Jill jumps in the back but climbs over to the front seat.
KENNY Hey!
JILL You can have the front on the way back.

They drive off. Mary stands outside the house, watching – her face is hard.

23 The car

ANDREW How are you, son?
KENNY Fine, Dad.
ANDREW How did the match go yesterday?
KENNY Good game. I scored.
ANDREW Once?
KENNY Just once.
ANDREW Did you win?
KENNY (*grinning*) Aye, we won.
ANDREW Great. How's my girl?
JILL Okay, Dad.
ANDREW How's school?
JILL It's fine.
ANDREW So we're all fine (*A pause, then he asks offhandedly*) How's your Mum?
JILL Just as usual.
ANDREW Still managing to get out and about?
JILL (*guardedly*) Now and then.
ANDREW Good! Car's a bit better than the bus, isn't it?
KENNY Sure is. Where we going then?
ANDREW Today – I'm going to call for a friend.
JILL A friend?
ANDREW Wait and see. And then we'll go places.

He leans forward and switches on the car radio. We cut to find Doreen in the seat beside Andrew. She is dark, slim, in her late twenties – enjoying the drive. Jill and Kenny eye her uneasily. Then Doreen opens her carrier bag and passes bags of crisps to the children – they receive them with friendly enough smiles. Andrew points Doreen to the glove department. She opens it and brings out cans of Coke. She holds them up for Jill and Kenny who grin and take them.

24 Loch Lomond

A scenic beauty-spot. Kenny, Jill, Doreen and Andrew are in a rowing-boat on the loch. The children are busy munching chocolate.

ANDREW (*unwinding a fishing line*) Will I bait it for you?
KENNY No, I'll do it. In a minute.
DOREEN You look a bit white.
KENNY I'm okay.
DOREEN You've had too much chocolate.

Kenny ruefully wraps his half Mars Bar back in the paper.

ANDREW Kenny – when I was about eight, my father took me fishing – it was up Loch Fyne or somewhere like that. And he told me, when it was in the water to keep it moving, you know, kid, the fish on it was worth swallowing. So I put it over...

He unwinds it over the side.

ANDREW ...and waved it up and down as far as my wee arms would stretch, and as fast as I could. And we must have been passing over a shoal, 'cos there was a great twitching and my Dad heaved it in. With the moving up and down I'd hooked a fish by the tail.
KENNY (*uninterested*) Do it again, Dad.
ANDREW You never know.
DOREEN Will I row?
JILL No.

The boat and its occupants are at rest. Then Andrew tries his arm movement.

ANDREW Nothing doing. D'you want to fish, Doreen?
DOREEN (*smiling*) Depends what for.
ANDREW In the water!
DOREEN I'll watch you.

Jill has caught the innuendo, and looks away. She rows furiously. Andrew is jerked back in his seat and splashed.

ANDREW Hey, steady on! Stop that! Jill!

25 A hotel bar

ANDREW How d'you think we're doing!
DOREEN What?
ANDREW With the kids?
DOREEN Fine. Don't worry. Take your time.
ANDREW (*managing a grin*) Then we'll give them a shout.

26 The loch side

Jill and Kenny are throwing stones aimlessly into the water.

KENNY Doreen . . .
JILL Well?

Kenny shrugs.

JILL You don't care?
KENNY No.
JILL I hate her. I hate her.
KENNY She's all right.
JILL What about Mum?
KENNY What about her?
JILL I want to go home.
KENNY You can't.
JILL We could hitch.

Kenny looks at her.

ANDREW (*distant voice*) Kenny! Jill! Come for lunch-*e*-on!

27 The hotel restaurant

They are at a table overlooking the loch. A waitress is clearing away. Jill's and Kenny's plates have only been toyed with.

ANDREW You should have said if you didn't want it.
KENNY Sorry, Dad.
JILL Too much stuffing ourselves.
DOREEN (*to Andrew*) I told you.
ANDREW (*to Doreen*) D'you want another beer?

DOREEN Are you having one?
ANDREW Ay.
DOREEN Okay. What about your children?
JILL I'm full, thanks.
DOREEN (*to Kenny*) Would you like a shandy?
KENNY I do drink beer now.

Doreen and Andrew give him a long look.

DOREEN Have one on me.

She looks for a waitress, holds up her arm and snaps a finger.

ANDREW What'll we do this afternoon?
KENNY Can I watch the football?
ANDREW Jeez – we're at Loch Lomond, son!
KENNY They've got a colour set in the lounge.
DOREEN (*to Andrew*) Let him; it's his day off.

28 The hotel lounge

Andrew and Kenny are watching the television.

ANDREW Mum still friends with that office bloke?
KENNY Who?
ANDREW George, is it?
KENNY Oh him?

Pause.

ANDREW Is she?
KENNY (*concentrating on the screen*) I don't know.
ANDREW What d'you think of Doreen?

Kenny gives a shrug.

ANDREW I've got quite friendly with her. Thought it was time you met her. She wanted to meet you.

There is a pause.

ANDREW Kenny.
KENNY What?
ANDREW You know you can leave school at Easter.
KENNY Ay.
ANDREW Just to let you know I wouldn't object. You've had your troubles there on the bookwork.

KENNY What would I do?

ANDREW There are jobs, Kenny. I don't say you should follow me and be a painter, but there are openings. Let me tell you, son, there's nothing like a bit of independence. I know.

29 The woods

Jill and Doreen are walking, a tension between them.

JILL Do you see Dad at the Works?

DOREEN Sometimes. I'm in my wee office, I'm a secretary to the Engineering Manager. Your Dad's outside mostly. Except in Trades Week, then he comes in with the Maintenance people. That's when I met him really. Jill, he's a great man.

JILL Is he?

DOREEN Yes, he is. What's your mother been telling you?

Jill doesn't answer.

DOREEN Because I've seen you looking at me when your Dad and me have been talking to each other. That's the way of it, then. Your mother forced your Dad out, and he's got a life to live, and at the moment I'm part of it. Okay?

JILL (*manages to say it*) Okay.

DOREEN I'll say this, I do know your Dad's a good man, Jill. People do get bogged down, with the best intentions. That's what happened to him.

JILL I'd say it's what happened to Mum too.

DOREEN (*ironic*) Is that so? (*Pause*) Is she missing him?

Jill doesn't answer.

DOREEN I'd say you and Kenny –

JILL What?

DOREEN Well, you've had a wee bit of brainwashing.

Jill is astonished.

30 The living-room

The same evening. Kenny, Jill and Gran are sitting at their places. Mary is returning to the scullery for the other dishes. Kenny and Jill are eyeing the pot with no enthusiasm.

GRAN So tell me about Loch Lomond. It's a long time since I was there.

KENNY Was that in the war, Gran?
GRAN I've been since the war, and don't be cheeky.

Mary brings two more pots with their lids on.

JILL Mum...
MARY What? It's your favourite – mince and beans and mash.

She removes the lids, and steam rises. Kenny and Jill look sickly.

GRAN I told you, Mary.
MARY Has he stuffed you again? Didn't you tell him? I told you your tea would be ready when you came back! You're going to get that inside you!
GRAN Wheesht! If they canna, they canna. What did he give you? Sweets, chocolates?
MARY Beer?
JILL (*pause*) A little... You should know by now, Mum.
MARY Well I don't know! It seems a perfectly reasonable thing for a mother to have her kids back for tea!
KENNY It's not worth going.
MARY Was it worth going? What kind of father does that to you! Healthy feeding, eh? Gran, c'mon.

She ladles out mince, baked beans and mash on to Gran's plate and her own. She puts the two empty plates in front of Kenny and Jill.

MARY If that's all you can take.

Silence, while Mary and Gran take a forkful.

MARY Was he alone?

Pause.

KENNY What d'you mean?
MARY You've said he took you to Loch Lomond, in a car. Just the three of you?

Silence. Mary puts down her fork.

JILL He had a friend.
MARY Male or female?
JILL A woman.
MARY How old?
JILL Don't know.
GRAN About your Mum's age?

JILL (*tense*) A good bit younger.
MARY Called?
JILL Doreen.
MARY Oh Doreen. How did you like her? Kenny, you've got eyes.
KENNY She was all right.
MARY So it was a *nice* day?
KENNY (*getting up*) Oh, for heaven's sake Mum! What d'you want me to say, it was a lousy day, I hated it, okay!

He pushes his chair back and makes for the door.

MARY Just say the truth. Tell me, I've been stuck here all day, so I'd like to know – anything wrong in that?
KENNY (*going out, angry, sarcastic*) Ve haff ways of makin' you talk!

His bedroom door is heard slamming.

GRAN Your father's right stupid!
MARY Leave it.
GRAN Fine example.
MARY Please, Mum.
GRAN Well.
MARY He shouldn't have left the table.

She toys with her food, then lays it down.

MARY Is this Doreen, Dad's bird?
JILL At the moment.
GRAN Were you speaking to her?
JILL Of course.
GRAN What about?
JILL Nothing! We just went rowing and fished.
GRAN (*to Mary*) Do you know who she is? Have you met her?
MARY No.
JILL She's at the Works.
GRAN (*knowing*) Oh.

Mary with a disapproving look at Gran, gets up and goes out after Kenny.

31 Kenny's room

Kenny stands at the window looking out. Mary comes in.

MARY Did you tell your Dad how well you've been doing at school?
KENNY Not really.

MARY Why?

KENNY (*shrugging*) He said I could leave at Easter.

MARY But they're letting you try for your Highers. Did you not tell him?

KENNY No.

MARY (*sarcastic*) And what career is he planning for you?

KENNY Oh Mum.

MARY What did your Dad say?

KENNY Nothing much. A bit about being independent.

MARY Come on through, Kenny. (*She is suddenly near to tears*) I'll let you off with your mince.

Kenny stands his ground.

MARY What am I to do with you? You're too big to hug.

KENNY I am.

32 The living-room

Kenny and Jill are doing their homework. Gran and Mary are in the scullery, washing up.

MARY Leave school? (*She is vexed and bitter*) I know what's in Andy's mind, he doesn't want to keep paying for him, he wants him to earn his own wages.

GRAN The one who matters is Kenny.

MARY (*upset*) Buf if Andy stops paying!

GRAN Don't upset yourself.

MARY I'm not upset.

GRAN It's these damn Sundays. Does he have to see them?

MARY I know, they put the clock back.

33 Jill's room

Jill sits, fully-dressed, cross-legged on the bed. She gets up and goes to the mantelpiece – all the animals have now been cleared from it. In their place stand two photos of Andrew and Mary. Jill moves to the chest of drawers and takes out her shoe box of animals. She begins setting them out on the mantelpiece – then suddenly sweeps them back into the box. She returns to her bed, clutching the animals.

34 A club bar

Andrew and Doreen are seated at an alcove table, with nearly empty glasses.

DOREEN Tricky.

ANDREW It is. But that's how it is. As long as I can keep friends with the kids, see them right. I talk more to them once a week than I did when I was living with them. D'you want another?

He takes out his wallet and glances at its contents.

DOREEN You've had an expensive day. Leave it, Andy.

ANDREW Sure?

DOREEN Ay.

ANDREW Separation's an expensive business. And it hurts more when I know she's using my money to run around with.

DOREEN Are you okay for the rest of the week?

ANDREW Oh ay. I live quiet. Oh thanks for the loan of the car.

DOREEN That's all right.

ANDREW It was real nice of you. You can keep the petrol that's left.

DOREEN I'll treasure it.

A pause.

ANDREW Doreen –

DOREEN No, you don't need to say anything more.

He looks sad.

DOREEN I quite enjoy being single.

ANDREW I used to dream, day-dream, that I'd walk out of the house, or she'd walk out, and I'd have the kids; and there'd be this beautiful woman . . . you know? Like you, or . . . And the four of us would have a great time. But it's not like that, not like a dream. Hard facts. I mean, who'd take me on?

DOREEN Somebody might, some day. I hope it happens.

He gives her a grin of thanks.

35 The living-room

It is late in the evening. Gran is alone, knitting, watching an old film on the box. The final music wells up. She looks at the clock on the mantelpiece, puts her knitting into her bag, gets up and goes out.

36 The hall

Gran takes her coat and hat from the peg, then goes to Kenny's door. She opens it.

GRAN Goodnight, Kenny my lad. I'm going home now.

37 Kenny's room

Kenny is reading a paperback in bed. He looks up and grins. The room is tidy.

KENNY Goodnight, Gran. Where did Mum go?
GRAN Oh, just out. Put your light out now, or you'll not be fit for school.
KENNY I'll finish my chapter.
GRAN Promise?
KENNY Ay.
GRAN Goodnight then.
KENNY Goodnight.

She shuts the door.

38 Jill's room

Jill is in bed with the light off. Her box of animals is on the floor by the bed. Gran opens the door, putting on her coat.

GRAN Are you asleep?
JILL No.

She sits up and switches on her light.

GRAN I'm off now. Will you be all right?
JILL Yes thanks.
GRAN What's thc box?
JILL Just my old animals.
GRAN Oh ay. Haven't seen them for a long time.
JILL I got tired of them.
GRAN Are you going to set them up again?
JILL I don't know. I just don't know.
GRAN (*giving her a look*) Are you sure you're okay?
JILL Aye. Where did Mum go?
GRAN Just to see someone. Goodnight, my wee lassie.
JILL Goodnight.
GRAN No sae wee now?

No answer from Jill.

GRAN Goodnight.

She shuts the door.

39 The club

Andrew and Doreen are sitting as before.

BARMAN Andy – your wife's here.

A look flashes between Doreen and Andrew.

DOREEN I'll go.
ANDREW No, you won't. (*To the barman*) Let her in.

The barman goes off. Andrew and Doreen wait.

ANDREW What's this for?
DOREEN Oh, God, I'm embarrassed.
ANDREW What for?

Mary comes to the table.

ANDREW Hello. Sit down.
MARY Can I talk to you?
ANDREW Why not? This is Doreen Shelty. Mary.

The two women give each other nods.

MARY I've been hearing about you.
DOREEN Oh really.
MARY From Jill and Kenny. (*To Andrew*) Can I talk to you about a few private things, Andrew?
DOREEN I'll go. (*With edge*) Nice to meet you Mary. I'll see you, Andy.
ANDREW All right.

Doreen gets up and goes without a look back.

MARY Nice of her.
ANDREW What's all this?
MARY You're looking well.
ANDREW I am well. You're looking all right too.
MARY (*abruptly*) Thanks.

A pause.

ANDREW So?
MARY These Sundays are no good, Andy. It's no good taking the kids out and sending them back to me too sick to have tea, from stuffing them with chocolate and beer.
ANDREW (*not interested*) Is that so?
MARY Andy, it's no skin off my nose, it's Jill and Kenny.

ANDREW (*softening*) I take the point.

MARY If you're taking them for the day, you give them tea. Ration them decently, and see they're home in time for schoolwork.

ANDREW Laying down the law, aren't you?

MARY These Sundays . . . are very disruptive. If you're not going to be responsible, we'll cut them out.

ANDREW We'll go to a lawyer then and see what the real law says. I've got to see my kids. I don't see them during the week.

MARY Can you not see their side?

ANDREW Ay, as much as you. I was thinking, actually, I've got a couple of rooms now, I could have them to stay on Saturdays.

Mary bristles.

ANDREW Kenny and me could go to the match, then Jilly could come and have tea with us and they could stay the night. I'll bring them back Sunday night.

MARY You can have them for holidays too then. A week's mid-term, two weeks coming up at Christmas, two at Easter, six weeks in summer, you can have the lot.

Andrew is not happy with this.

MARY You and me have got to come to an arrangement, Andy. And I'll tell you what Kenny didn't tell you: he's doing very well at school so he's not leaving.

ANDREW How well?

MARY *Very* well.

ANDREW It's not for you to decide.

MARY He'll have a better start than you did!

ANDREW I'm not ashamed of myself. I've done not bad, Mary.

They pause, and look at each other with mistrust, defiance.

MARY Must it be every week?

ANDREW Ay. I've got to see they're surviving.

MARY (*getting up*) Oh, they're doing that, Andy. (*Spells it out*) The kids are okay!

40 Kenny's room

Kenny is asleep. The room is dark.

JILL (*from her room, screams*) Kenny! Kenny!

Kenny wakes up, looks up, alert.

KENNY (*shouts*) What?
JILL (*voice*) Kenny.

He gets up quickly and goes out.

41 Jill's room

Jill is crouched on the floor in a corner. Her animals are scattered round her. Kenny comes in.

KENNY What's wrong?
JILL (*shaking*) I've taken . . . I've taken . . .

He goes to her and forces her hand open. He takes a pill bottle from her.

JILL Mum's sleeping-pills.
KENNY You stupid . . .! What did you take them for? How many?
JILL Five.
KENNY Five!!?
JILL (*weeping*) I don't know . . . I don't want to die. I don't want to die!
KENNY You won't! I'll go next door, get Mrs Oliver.
JILL Get Mum.
KENNY Shurrup now. She'll phone.

Jill closes her eyes, shaking.

42 Council block

We see a taxi draw up – Andrew and Mary quickly getting out and racing up the path to the house. An ambulance can be heard approaching through the night.

43 Jill's room

Jill is fast asleep on the floor, with a blanket over her. Kenny is there, and Mrs Oliver. The door is flung open, and Mary and Andrew come in.

MARY Where is she?
ANDREW What happened?

They bend down to Jill.

MARY Jill my darling?
KENNY Your sleeping pills.
ANDREW Jill! Jill! Has she been sick?

The ambulance men come in with a stretcher.

MARY Oh, when did she . . .?
KENNY Mind, Dad – here's the ambulance . . .

We cut to:

44 Hospital cubicle

Jill is lying back, comfortable. Mary and Andrew are visiting.

ANDREW We've all got our lives to live, Jill, and so have you.
MARY We all make mistakes.
ANDREW I was speaking to the doctor. He said that maybe you need to talk more about things.
MARY Things that worry you.
ANDREW Everybody's got problems, Jill. We all need to talk. Will you do that?
JILL (*faint smile*) I'll try.

Mary and Andrew's eyes meet.

MARY Leave it, Andrew.
ANDREW (*getting up*) I think Kenny's waiting to see you. So you'll be home tomorrow, and I'll see you at the weekend.
JILL Okay Dad.
MARY I'll come for you in the morning. Bring your things.
JILL Right.

They go out through the curtains. Kenny comes in.

JILL Hello.
KENNY Hello. How are you?
JILL Fine.
KENNY (*pausing*) You're stupid.
JILL I know. What are they doing?
KENNY She's blaming him, he's blaming her.

Jill's face falls.

KENNY Come on Jill! Tomorrow I'll play you tennis.

If Only
David Cook

The Cast

Brian, *aged fifteen*
Micky, *his dead friend – voice only in some scenes*
Policeman
Vicar – *voice only*
Brian's mother
Brian's father
Lynn, *his sister*
Dr West, *the family doctor*
Bus conductress
Jan } *girls at disco*
Trish }
Caretaker at Brian's school
Old-age pensioner
Mrs Thompson, *Micky's mother*
Mary, *Micky's sister*

An asterisk * indicates a flashback scene.

If Only

1 A sequence of camera shots

Silence is shattered by a sudden burst of pop music to coincide with the appearance of an eyelid blinking open and a whole eyeball filling the screen.

A cemetery. The camera is looking up from inside a very deep grave to see a fishing line and hook dangling down. Heads can be made out peering into the grave, and the voice over of Brian's mother is heard. "If only he'd cry."

A river. A camera shot from under water. Reeds cover the lens and a fishing line and hook dangle down. With soft organ music in the background we hear the vicar's voice: "Man that is born of woman hath but a short time to live, and is cut down. Ashes to ashes, dust to dust . . ." We see Micky's body being hooked out of the river by a policeman with a long pole.

The graveside. Brian is looking down, holding a lump of clay. A shot from inside the grave watches the clay falling towards the lens. The voice of Brian's Dad is heard over: "My son cry? He won't cry. Not him."

2 Brian's bedroom

A shot of Brian lying, eyes open, impassive on his bed. Loud music in the background. The camera closes on a snapshot pinned to a wallboard. There are many other pictures and pin-ups, but this one is of Micky and Brian together. We never see Micky too clearly. He is always at a distance, turned half away, in shadow, or slightly out of focus. We always want to know more of what he looks like.

MICKY (*voice*) We've got sixty more years at the very least. By the time we're forty, people'll probably live to an average of a hundred years.

3 Bus station*

Brian and Micky are leaning against a wall, watching the buses come and go.

BRIAN Good luck to them.
MICKY What are you doing to do with all those hours?
BRIAN I dunno. Find something interesting.
MICKY (*parrots*) "Something interesting"! You're like a scratched LP that's stuck. What's more interesting than making a pile of money?
BRIAN Lots of things.
MICKY Name one.

A fat lady is in danger of being flattened by a bus. She does a little run.

BRIAN Money can't stop you being flattened by a bus.

4 Brian's bedroom

Music playing. The camera is on Brian's face – he blinks. Something is wrong. The record has stuck and he gets up to change it. His mother is heard shouting from outside.

MOTHER (*voice*) Are you all right? Brian, will you answer me? That noise is disturbing Mrs Marshall. A woman that age shouldn't have to put up with punk at three in the afternoon. What's wrong with those earphone things?

Brian has the record off. He freezes to listen to another – interior – voice.

MICKY (*voice*) When am I going to get my earphones back, Brian?
BRIAN Soon.

5 The kitchen

Brian, his mother, father and his sister, Lynn, sit round the table, eating in silence. Looks are exchanged as Brian scoffs his food while reading the New Musical Express. *The others are clearly on edge.*
After a long silence –

MOTHER Haven't lost your appetite. (*Pause, then to Dad*) He is hungry.

Dad gives her a look. Another long silence. Then mother asks a general question.

MOTHER When was it we relaxed our rule about no reading during meals? (*Another look from Dad*) Well, I wasn't sent a copy of the new Standards of Behaviour Agreement.

Brian's eyes have never left the paper. He now rises slowly to his feet, his mouth still full of food. He reaches across the table, takes a large slice of bread and leaves the room. Lynn and Dad look at Mother, who stands and starts to clear things away.

MOTHER I don't see why the whole of civilisation as we know it should take a step back, just because someone has died.

She has lifted Lynn's plate and is about to remove it, but Lynn retrieves it.

LYNN When I've finished eating, Mum, I'll inform you, just as I have at every mealtime since I was four, and could pronounce the magic words, "Thank you for my tea. Please may I get down?"

MOTHER And you're not too big yet to be . . .

LYNN Put across your knee? And never will be, if you keep whipping the food away, just as my taste buds have finally summoned up enough courage.

MOTHER What's wrong with it?

LYNN Nothing. It's a miracle of culinary achievement. What's its name?

MOTHER The butcher didn't tell me, and I didn't like to ask.

DAD It's nearly two weeks. (*Lynn doesn't understand*) Brian.

LYNN (*shrugs*) He'll have to talk to someone sooner or later. Unless, of course, he squats down in a corner, faces the wall, and goes quietly and irretrievably insane. Has been known – in severe cases.

DAD Cases of what?

LYNN Grief. Severe cases of grief. He's in mourning for Micky. Stricken with grief. Takes people in funny ways. Extremely unfunny, some of the ways it takes them.

MOTHER Nothing very humorous about the way it took poor Mrs Wilson. That was really sad. Christmas Eve two years ago. They had to bring her back from right over the other side of King's Heath. She'd been running around the streets in her nightdress and banging on people's doors, calling for her little boy.

LYNN Darren.

MOTHER Banging on the doors, and screaming out his name. And two months before, he'd died in her own house of meningitis.

DAD But that was her child.

MOTHER Her only child. She's still not got over it.

DAD Right. Her only child. Micky was just a friend.

LYNN Best friend.

DAD It's not the same.

LYNN Only friend, it seems like.

DAD It's not the same. I mean, this not going to school and not talking to anyone, is just mad.

LYNN So is going to strangers' houses, calling for your little boy, when you watched him die.

6 Brian's bedroom

Evening. Brian is lying on the bed. Micky talks to him inside his head. When Brian answers, he speaks aloud.

MICKY (*voice*) So what are you scared of, Brian?

BRIAN Dunno.

MICKY (*voice*) It's yourself you're scared of, isn't it?

7 The riverside*

Brian and Micky are fishing.

MICKY You always did think too much. Think yourself out of existence sometimes. I've watched you. Seen you wondering if you're really there. There are two kinds of people in this world, Bri, those who do things, and those who just think about doing them. You live through me. All your life, you'll have to stick close to me just to be where the action is.

BRIAN Some action!

MICKY I could never sit, waiting to be asked if I'd like to join in things. Only time you talk is when I force you by asking questions. You're not exactly a mine of information.

8 The landing outside Brian's room

Dad, listening, hears Brian inside talking to Micky.

BRIAN OK. Pass. Ask me another. What would you like to know?

MICKY (*voice*) Well, for starters, when am I going to get my earphones back?

BRIAN (*whispers*) Soon.

He flings the earphones down on the bed, rushes for the door, opens it and almost collides with Dad.

BRIAN Soon!

9 Brian's bedroom

Dad watches Brian rush down the stairs, then walks into the bedroom. He looks around slowly, sees the wallboard. He takes down the snap of Brian and Micky, looks at it, thinks, looks as though he is about to tear it up, then decides not to. He sits on the edge of the bed.

10 Doctor's office

Dr West is the family doctor. He is extremely embarrassed at having to conduct this interview.

DR WEST Come in, Brian, do come in, take a seat, how're you feeling? (*Brian shrugs*) Yes, well, you've had a shock, shaken you up a bit; I expect your parents are a bit shaken too, I wouldn't wonder, seeing *you* having been so shaken, in a state of shock. Is that the trouble, do you suppose? (*Brian shrugs*) Only to be expected in the circumstances, unhappy time all round for everyone; no reason to stay away from school for ever, though, is there? You look healthy enough, how's the girl-friend – wosser-name? (*Pause*) No special girl at the moment, then?

Brian shakes his head.

DR WEST Pity, never mind, expect there will be, plenty of time, time for all that. And you do like girls, don't you?

Long pause. Brian just looks at him.

DR WEST I expect your parents are worrying over nothing, don't you? (*Slight pause*) Difficult time of life yours, no longer one of the lads, not yet one of the chaps, get some funny notions at your age. Had 'em myself. Still, as long as you like girls, that's the main thing, everything else comes out in the wash. I think I can set your parents' minds at rest, don't you?

Brian nods. He gets slowly to his feet. He crosses to the doctor's desk, stands looking at him, winks and leaves the room. Close-up on Dr West's perplexed face.

11 Street scene

Brian is walking down the street, listening to Micky's voice.

MICKY (*voice*) We haven't lived yet, Bri. It worries me sometimes, just thinking about what we've got to look forward to. The responsibility of having a good time out of life. Making the most of it all depresses me, do you know that? I sit in the bath, staring at my belly button, and start to get hot flushes. I look at that wrinkled little crater, filled with fluff and congealed rice pudding and think "what's it all for? I'm fifteen years, two months and three days old. When am I going to start living?"

Brian hears a bus coming, but is some way from the stop. He runs and jumps into it as it is pulling away.

12 The bus

Brian is seated on the top deck. The conductress stands waiting for his fare. He holds out a coin. She looks at the coin, then back at him.

CONDUCTRESS Where to? I asked you where you want to go to, man.

He indicates 30p.

CONDUCTRESS I ain't taking that money. Either you state your destination, or I chuck you off at the next traffic light, OK?

Brian taps two closed fingers on his mouth and makes dumb signs. The conductress is taken in.

CONDUCTRESS Sorry, love. I'll give you 30p-worth. You just get off when you feel like it, OK?

Brian smiles at her and she smiles back. He turns to look out of the window.

MICKY (*voice*) You know something?
BRIAN Not a lot.
MICKY (*voice*) You're a creep. Persecuting the minorities.
BRIAN Bossy bus conductresses aren't in a minority. They rule the world.

The conductress is now lecturing a lady passenger.

CONDUCTRESS If it says Town Centre on the front, that's where we're going lady. If we were going to Botley Park, it would say Botley Park, and I'd be working overtime.

Brian looks out of the window and we cut to –

13 The disco*

Loud music, distorting mirrors, and flashing lights. Brian and Micky enter, blinking at the lights. During the dialogue they buy and drink Cokes.

MICKY This is the life. What do you think?
BRIAN Not bad.
MICKY Not bad! What do you mean "not bad"? It only opened last week.
BRIAN Never mind. Perhaps they'll close it down soon and build a real one. You going to dance?
MICKY Not with you. I'm choosy.

We see two girls dancing together. They have seen the boys.

MICKY Shall we split them up?
BRIAN Not yet. I'm trying to decide which one's yours.
MICKY Why do I do it? Why did I bring you? You'll stand there all night, stuffing your face, and then complain that you didn't enjoy yourself. What am I doing here?
BRIAN You mean *there*.

We cut back to –

14 The bus

Brian is still gazing out of the window.

MICKY (*voice*) You what?
BRIAN There.
MICKY (*voice*) Come again.
BRIAN You mean, what are you doing *there*? You're there now, not here.
MICKY (*voice*) Where am I?
BRIAN I don't know. You tell me.

Brian sees that the conductress has been watching him talk out loud. He gets to his feet slowly, then quickens his movements as the bus slows down enough for him to jump off. As the bus pulls away, the conductress calls to him.

CONDUCTRESS Hey, I remember faces, boy.
MICKY (*voice*) Haven't I seen you before?

Brian smiles, remembering.
Cut back to –

15 The disco*

Brian, Micky, Jan and Trish are at the same table drinking Coke. Micky speaks to Trish.

MICKY Excuse me, Madam, but haven't I seen you before?
TRISH Before what?
MICKY Didn't you star in that film? What was it called now?
BRIAN Lassie? (*A look from Trish*) The Incredible Hulk? (*Another look*) The Blob?
MICKY Shut up. No, honest, I'm never wrong about a face. I remember yours distinctly. You were wearing fishnet tights, a very short skirt, and eyelashes out to here.
BRIAN Is that all?
JAN She was probably selling the icecream.
BRIAN That's it! He'd run down the aisle, and *you'd* run out of Raspberry Ripple. So he said "keep the change". He's very good, isn't he? He never forgets a face.
JAN You're both still at school, aren't you?
MICKY How can you tell?
JAN It's all in the eyes, a sort of glint, hopeful, like. Either that or you've both got dirty minds.
BRIAN Could both be true?
MICKY (*to Jan*) And what do they call you?
JAN A statistic.
MICKY Is it painful?
JAN Only on Fridays.
BRIAN Are you a vital statistic, or just the common or garden variety?
JAN Dead common. There are millions of us. You could be one soon if you play your cards right.
TRISH You mean "get your cards". Right?

The girls laugh.

JAN Why do you always give it away? Come on, let's dance.

The girls stand.

MICKY No, no. Sit down. I haven't got it yet, 'cos I'm thick.
TRISH Not with a name like Micky, surely?

Brian takes Jan's hand.

BRIAN That was cruel – to christen a baby and land it with a name like that.

JAN What name?

BRIAN Social Security.

JAN That's my friend. I'm called Supplementary Benefit.

16 Mrs Thompson's living room

The flat is on the sixth floor of a large block. The curtains of the room are drawn. The only light is from an open fire. Micky's mother, Mrs Thompson, sits, staring into the fire. Mary, his younger sister, stands by the window, holding the curtains open and looking out.

MARY He's there again. Micky's friend. He's standing outside again.

MRS T (*flat tone*) I've told you. Close the curtains.

17 Block of flats

Brian is standing below, watching as Mary lets the curtains close. He slowly lowers his head.

MICKY (*voice*) Who's the most important person in your life?

BRIAN Father Christmas.

MICKY (*voice*) Seriously.

18 The riverside*

BRIAN You can't talk seriously about that. It's daft.

MICKY Why?

BRIAN Well, sometimes it's one person, sometimes another.

MICKY Not with me.

BRIAN OK. You're obviously dying to tell me. Who's the unlucky lady.

MICKY (*laughing*) Me Mum.

BRIAN Idiot!

MICKY No, it's important. I've been thinking about it. She's all right. And she's had a hard life. She was great when I was a baby.

BRIAN How do you know? You can't remember that far back.

MICKY I can remember when I was two, thinking I'd found some sweets, and swallowing the whole packet of laxatives.

BRIAN Yeah, that would leave a lasting impression.

MICKY It's difficult now to . . . you know . . . show her you like her. (*Short pause*) Do you find that?

BRIAN I don't know your mum very well. (*Laughs*) She might get the wrong idea.

MICKY First thing on the list when I make my packet – buy her a house with a garden.

BRIAN What's second?

MICKY A Rolls Royce Silver Cloud with stereophonic upholstery. And speaking of stereo . . .

BRIAN "When am I going to get my earphones back?"

19 The kitchen

Brian comes in from outside to find his mother laying the table. He gets to the door to the hall, but her voice stops him.

MOTHER Mr Atkins rang. Wanted to know where you were. He says he can't cover up for you with the Attendance Officer any longer. (*Brian turns*) Why don't you go back? The longer you stay away, the worse it'll be when you do go. (*He moves to leave*) I haven't finished. (*He turns back*) He wanted to know if you were doing any work on your own. Said it might help to take your mind off things. And did you realise they might want to see your school reports when it's time for you to get a job? I had to tell him we don't know how you spend your time during the day, that you just come in for your meals and won't even talk to us. Brian. (*Pause – suddenly sad*) I keep thinking he'll ring the doorbell. Micky. Just turn up, looking for you. I can't believe it's really happened. Can't get used to it yet.

He is looking at her.

MICKY (*voice*) It's difficult now to show her you like her.

Brian reacts and runs out of the kitchen.

20 Brian's bedroom

Brian enters quickly, closes the door, and leans against it. A dog can be heard barking in the distance. Brian rushes to the window, closes it and draws the curtains.

MICKY (*voice*) It's struggling, I tell you.

21 The riverside*

A small dog is struggling in the river and seems to be in difficulties. Some small children stand on the bank throwing stones towards (but not too close to) the dog. Brian is worried that Micky might do something silly.

BRIAN Dogs can swim. Leave it.

MICKY It's exhausted. It's going to go under.

22 Brian's bedroom

Brian is biting the back of his hand. He lowers the hand and speaks almost inaudibly.

BRIAN Come back.

23 The riverside*

The small dog is on the bank shaking itself dry. A well dressed middle-aged woman wraps a blanket round the dog, picks it up, cuddles it, but all the time looking at Brian, who watches her. He turns away. A policeman with a long pole, is fishing Micky's jacket out of the water. An ambulance man gives Micky artificial respiration. An ambulance siren is heard.

MICKY (*voice*) All your life, you'll have to stick close to me to be where the action is.

24 The school yard

Brian is staring into the school hall, watching some Old Time Dancing. He moves stealthily into the school, going along the corridor by the caretaker's office.

25 The corridor

The office door is open. Brian sees a bunch of keys on the table, takes them and makes off. He runs straight into the caretaker's arms.

CARETAKER You're not over sixty, are you? An OAP? One of our Senior Citizens? My word, you've aged well! Perhaps you've come to collect one of our Old Tyme Dancers, have you? Or deliver? You found one leapfrogging on the bypass, did you? Brought her back, come to replace her within the community situation? No? A foreigner, eh? That's it... Remedial English... Thursdays; you're on the wrong night. Speech Therapy? The Margaret Thatcher Voice Improvement Class, and bring your own greengrocery for the plummy bits.

Brian struggles but his shoulders are held. The caretaker doesn't see the keys.

CARETAKER No! You come with me. They're always short of men. Had me in there last week, I walked home a cripple! Are you conversant with Roger de Coverley? The Military Two-Step? Strip the Willow? The Gay Gordons? No? Not even the Gay Gordons? Here! I'll show you.

He goes to take hold of Brian's arms and lift them above his head. Brian has hidden the keys in his pocket. The caretaker hums the music of the Gay Gordons and takes a couple of steps, but is interrupted by the crashing noise of breaking crockerey. Brian's head jerks in the direction of the sound.

CARETAKER There they go again! All the rock cakes gone for a Burton.

Brian seizes his chance and dashes away.

CARETAKER Here! Come back!

He starts after Brian but is stopped by a voice from the hall.

OAP Mr Jackson! Mr Jackson!
CARETAKER I heard. I'm just on my way to fetch the tow-rope.

26 A classroom

Brian is outside the door. He turns the key, opens the door and goes in.

MICKY (*voice*) There are people who do things, and those who just think about doing them.

27 The riverside*

MICKY It's struggling, I tell you.
BRIAN So what? It's a dog. It's not even your dog. All you're after is your picture in the local paper.

Micky is taking his shoes off.

BRIAN Stop trying to prove you're a hero. It's thirty foot deep in the middle, and the most you've ever swum is one width of breaststroke down at the shallow end.
MICKY You go in, then, you're the swimmer. Here's a chance to practise your life-saving.

Brian is physically trying to stop Micky from going in the water.

BRIAN If it was a child I would, but dogs can swim. It's not worth the risk.

MICKY (*pushing him away*) What's the point of being alive if you don't take the odd risk?

He starts to walk into the water.

BRIAN (*getting very angry*) Is this what you call being where the action is? It's pathetic. You're mad. Do you know that?

MICKY So you keep telling me.

BRIAN Next thing, you'll be wanting to give it the kiss of life.

Micky takes no notice and goes on wading in. Brian starts to kick his shoes off.

BRIAN All right, all right! You win. I'll do it. Come back. I'll go in. At least I can swim.

Micky is waist high in the water.

MICKY Don't worry. It's only a dog.

28 The classroom

The faint background sound of old-time dance music. Brian is standing by his open desk, holding something he has taken from it. As we hear Micky's voice over, the camera pans down so we see clearly what it is: a certificate for lifesaving, awarded to Brian Watson.

MICKY (*voice*) There are those who do things, and those who just think about doing them.

We see a close-up of the certificate being torn into small pieces and the pieces dropping to the floor.

29 Mrs Thompson's living room

Mrs Thompson is sitting close to the fire almost as before. The living room door is open; Mary can be heard at the front door.

MARY (*voice*) She won't see anyone. Won't go out.

A pause. Then Mrs Thompson looks up.

MRS T Has he gone?

Mary is at the door of the living-room. She has a brown paper bag.

MARY He brought these.

MRS T (*looks away*) What are they?

MARY Photos, earphones for the stereo, some school work, a football scarf. These look like poems.

MRS T (*staring into the fire*) What made him think I'd want them?

She turns back towards Mary. Then we see that Brian has come in and stands behind Mary, just inside the living-room door. Mrs Thompson stares at him. A pause. She speaks to Mary.

MRS T I told you I didn't want to see him. Get him out.

Brian does not move.

MRS T Give him those back. (*To Brian*) What made you think I'd want them? I'm trying to forget him. I don't need any reminders.

Mary holds out the things to Brian, but he won't take them.

MRS T I don't want them.

Brian shakes his head.

MRS T Bring them here.

Brian does so and she starts to put them on the fire.

MARY (*to Brian*) We burned all his clothes and things.

MRS T If I'd given them away, I might have seen someone in the street, wearing them. (*Watches flames*) I said I didn't want to see you. Have you come to say you're sorry? Exchange a few words of sympathy and go back to playing football? Or is it fishing? I've lost count of the number of people who've knocked on that door . . . people who hardly knew him, had never spoken to him, some who didn't even like him, because he answered them back. They climb up five flights of stairs to say they're sorry. Sorry! *They're* sorry! (*Turns to fire*) "Sorry, mum. Won't do it again." (*Biting her lip*) And he won't will he?

MARY Don't, Mum. Please.

MRS T (*to Brian*) You'd better go.

Brian turns to the door and has his hand on the handle. He rests his forehead on the door and looks at the floor. There is a very long pause. He is moving his lips, trying to form words. He mouths "Help . . . me". Mrs Thompson slowly gets up and goes to him. She stands looking at him, takes his shoulders and turns him round to face her. She places her hand under his chin and lifts his face up. He is crying. For a second it seems that she is going to hug him to her. Then she suddenly swipes him across the face. Brian is stunned and disbelieving.

MRS T You're alive, and he's dead, and you ask me for help! I thought you came here because you were sorry for me, not for yourself. Micky liked you more than anyone else; I can't think why. All right, so you've had a shock. Your best friend can't come out to play any more. That's it. Finished. End of story, end of a life. Fifteen years. Better not to have had them. Better not to have known him. You'll leave school, get a job, take home your first pay packet. Court someone, get married, present your mother with grandchildren, and watch them grow up. So now you understand why I can't take you feeling sorry for yourself, not just at the moment. Why I don't want you standing in my living room, crying and asking for help. There are over a thousand kids at your school. One of them should be able to replace Micky for you. (*Pausing*) You saw more of him than I did over the last few years. Be grateful for that. I was just his mother – wasn't even given a chance to tell him. I . . . I'd carried him around inside me for nine months, and now I can't even remember the last time we touched each other. He was past the age to be hugged and kissed. I wanted to hold him, wanted to tell him he was still mine, but I didn't. Didn't dare. Didn't want to embarrass him. No fear of that now. (*She breaks down angrily*) You don't even get the chance to tell them you love them. Why? Why is that? And why him? Can you tell me? (*Brian shakes his head*) Don't come here again. I don't want his things, don't want the memory of him. It only makes me angry.

She is sobbing pitifully.

Brian moves slowly towards the door, then turns.

BRIAN He told me you were the most important person in his life. He was going to buy you a house with a garden.

He goes. Slowly Mrs Thompson crosses to the window, draws back the curtains and looks out.

30 Block of flats

Evening. Brian comes out of the block and begins to walk away. Mrs Thompson is at the window, but Brian does not look up. Young lads kick a football which goes right across Brian's path. He kicks it, looks up at the window and then he joins in the game.

Consequences

Leonard Kingston

The Cast

Russell Summers, *a teacher*
Berenice Summers, *his wife*
Paul, *their seventeen-year-old son*
Anne, *their sixteen-year-old daughter*
Liza, *her school friend, the same age*
Maureen Hollander, *Liza's mother*
Ted Hollander, *Liza's father*
Park-keeper
Mr Arbuthnot, *Park Superintendent*
Friend, *at University*

Consequences

Part One

1 The Summers' house: living-room

Russell Summers, fortyish, with glasses, leather patches on the elbows of his sports jacket, is seated at a very untidy desk. He is trying to work against a barrage of noise above him. Obviously hardened to such interruptions, he gives a rather absent-minded shout without looking up.

RUSSELL Quiet!

He is answered almost immediately by a particularly heavy bump. Roused, he springs up and runs a few steps into the hall.

2 The hall

RUSSELL What's happening up there?

Berenice, his wife – a thin, wearied, over-neat woman who tends to dominate her husband – pokes her head out of the kitchen, her hands covered with flour.

BERENICE (*mildly irritated*) What?
RUSSELL (*gesticulating*) Upstairs!
BERENICE It's only Anne. With Liza.
RUSSELL Liza?
BERENICE (*impatient*) Her new friend. You know. The dark-haired one.
RUSSELL (*bawling at another thump*) Anne!
BERENICE Anne! Your father's trying to work!

Russell has already angrily begun mounting the stairs. Music can be heard.

3 The snooker-room

Russell flings open the door. A three-quarter size snooker table is pushed back to one side, but we see very little of that. Anne, a large cheerful girl, has just completed a jump, or is just finishing, on all fours, head down. Near, watching, is Liza Hollander, a smaller, prettier girl. Both are sixteen and in school uniform.

RUSSELL Anne!

ANNE (*untroubled, maintaining her pose*) Ye-es?

RUSSELL What the hell are you up to?

ANNE A handstand to bridge.

RUSSELL A what?

ANNE (*springing back to her feet neatly, breathing a little, but triumphant*) There! That's fitness, dear!

RUSSELL I'm trying to work down there! A pile of marking this high. What's this all in aid of?

ANNE The school gymnastics display, Dad. Liza and I – we're partners. So we have to practise, don't we.

RUSSELL Well! (*Restrained by convention, half smiles, half scowls at Liza, who is still mildly scared. But looking at Liza he has seen the snooker table behind her. His voice is now choked with rage.*) And why have you moved my snooker table?

ANNE To give ourselves room.

RUSSELL You have no right –

ANNE But you wouldn't want us kicking lumps out of it, would you?

RUSSELL I've told you –

ANNE Oh, come off it, Dad. Here, let me show you an Arab spring.

RUSSELL (*handing her off as she bounds forward*) You can get downstairs and help your mother make supper.

ANNE (*retreating to door but wagging a finger at him*) Now, now, that's interference with the liberty of the individual.

RUSSELL (*moving after her, shouting*) Get downstairs!

With an amused yelp she retreats down the stairs, while Russell, moving out onto the landing after her, turns to push open the nearest door.

4 Paul's room

The music swells out as Russell pokes his head around the door.

RUSSELL Paul!

Paul, dressed in scruffy school uniform is half lying on his bed and scribbling in an exercise book. Textbooks cover the floor; loudspeakers and wires fill the rest of the room. He looks up at his father's entrance.

RUSSELL You can turn that racket down.

PAUL I'm doing homework.
RUSSELL Then stop doing it! Come in here.

Paul begins to rise, sighing heavily, and leans over to turn down the music, slightly.

RUSSELL Quicker!

Paul rolls his eyes in exasperation, but follows Russell.

5 The snooker-room

Russell strides back into the snooker-room, talking, school-masterly, pompous, as he goes.

RUSSELL Now I want you to move the snooker table back to its correct position. Right? Correctly aligned, levelled up. Can I trust you, Paul, to do that?
PAUL (*surly*) Oh, sure.
RUSSELL Linda here . . .
LIZA (*almost inaudibly*) Liza.
RUSSELL What? Who?
LIZA (*clearing her throat*) Liza!
RUSSELL (*looking at her severely*) You don't mind helping Paul?
LIZA No.
RUSSELL (*muttering under his breath*) Bloody children.

Russell exits. Paul sniggers; Liza smiles warily at him. They start moving the table.

6 The kitchen

It is clean, neat and fairly modern. Berenice is rolling out dough. Anne is sprawled in the winged kitchen chair – Russell's chair at all meals – leaning back, a foot up against the table leg, flipping through a magazine she has obviously just snatched up. Russell is coming through the door, still ruffled.

BERENICE (*sourly*) Did you send her down to help me?
RUSSELL (*mutters*) Lazy creature!
ANNE (*reading on happily*) I'm waiting to be told what to do.
BERENICE I don't want her here cluttering up my kitchen.
RUSSELL She's not going back upstairs.
ANNE (*throwing down the magazine*) Oh! But Liza's up there alone with Paul. Are you sure she's safe?

RUSSELL Completely. Sit down.

ANNE You know what young men are like.

RUSSELL (*slightly humorous*) I think we can trust our Paul to exercise proper restraint.

Anne is casually dipping her fingers into the fruit laid out for the pie.

BERENICE And stop that!

Anne mocks big-eyed innocence as she pops a slice of fruit into her mouth.

7 The snooker-room

Liza, wide-eyed, is watching Paul in a constrained silence. The snooker table is now back in the centre of the room. Paul is moving a small spirit level around on the table top, not looking at Liza but probably aware that she is looking at him.

LIZA (*timidly breaking the silence*) What's that?

PAUL (*gruffly*) Spirit level.

LIZA Oh . . .

PAUL Has to be exactly level. That's why you shouldn't have moved it.

LIZA I'm sorry. Anne didn't say –

PAUL (*working, head down*) She wouldn't!

LIZA Your Dad's very keen is he?

PAUL Yes.

Another small silence.

LIZA (*timidly again*) Do *you* play?

PAUL Yes.

LIZA Who wins?

PAUL He does. Usually.

LIZA Ah . . .

PAUL (*a slow grin coming*) Because I let him. He gets in a temper if he doesn't.

LIZA (*still shyly*) You go to St Olave's, don't you?

PAUL Mm.

LIZA Does your dad teach at St Olave's?

PAUL Him? He's not good enough for our school.

Liza laughs.

PAUL No. He teaches at the technical college.

LIZA (*grinning*) Must be frightening having a teacher for a father.

PAUL (*grinning, tipping a few balls out onto the table*) Oh yer. A hundred lines if you don't wash behind your ears. Like a go?

LIZA Could I?

PAUL (*nods, handing her the cue*) You'll miss it.

LIZA Bet I don't (*bearing down on ball quickly*).

PAUL (*laughing*) No! That's the wrong ball! The white one! (*Almost choking with laughter, as she spars with cue*) And you don't hold it like that!

His arms flail around hers as she leans over the table, unsteadily and giggling.

8 The living-room

Russell is at his desk again – there is a tremendous thump above his head.

RUSSELL (*jumping up*) What the bloody! . . .

9 The snooker-room

Liza is on the floor, looking up, dismayed but still grinning. She has fallen off the table.

10 The hall and stairs

Russell is striding to the foot of the stairs.

RUSSELL What the . . .?

Paul is halfway down the stairs, stopping, smiling.

PAUL It's all right, Dad.

Liza edges down past him, giving a pale smile to Russell. Russell stares from one innocent face to the other, slightly baffled. Liza slips into the kitchen.

11 The kitchen

Supper. They are all eating a mixed grill. Russell is at the head of the table in his wing chair. He has some exercise books at the side of his plate. He eats with one hand, marks with speed and precision with the other – writing on and off as he talks, his mind half on the talk, half on his work. Berenice sits quietly, pained, bored throughout.

RUSSELL I'm all for physical exercise. In its proper place. Most young people take far too little. Far too keen on lying about listening to decadent pop music.

ANNE Sock it to him, Pops!

PAUL Mike Oldfield, Dad, is not decadent.

RUSSELL Isn't he? Well, a few Arab . . . what were they?

ANNE Arab springs.

RUSSELL A few Arab springs . . .

ANNE He'd never manage, Dad. He's not fit enough!

PAUL Thank you, fatty.

RUSSELL Would do you . . .

ANNE Fat? This is pure muscle! Hard as steel! (*Banging her stomach*)

PAUL Ha, hah!

RUSSELL (*loudly*) Am I *never* to be allowed to finish a sentence in this house?

PAUL No Dad. It's a life sentence here with us! Didn't anyone ever tell you?

ANNE Boom boom!

RUSSELL Very funny! But if you spent half . . .

PAUL Tell me, Dad. Don't your pupils object to getting their homework returned to them covered in bacon fat?

ANNE Yuk, yuk.

PAUL No, it's oink oink!

ANNE (*banging knife on the table*) Boom boom!

ERENICE Oh, be your age! Both of you!

There is an immediate drop in temperature, though Anne and Paul manage a grin.

RUSSELL Yes. Quite right. (*Looking at Liza*) I'm quite sure Lind – er –

ANNE Liza, Dad. As in Liza Minelli.

RUSSELL Well, I'm sure Liza's parents wouldn't allow such disgusting noises at their meal table.

Anne and Paul grin at Liza. Berenice takes no interest.

RUSSELL (*searching for a question*) What does your father . . . do . . . Liza?

LIZA Works in the park.

RUSSELL Oh. A park-keeper.

LIZA Yes.

RUSSELL Very interesting job.

PAUL No need to sneer, dad.

Russell is taken aback.

RUSSELL (*astonished*) Who was sneering?

PAUL (*going very red as all eyes are turned on him*) Well, I mean, well, in these days of pollution . . . and destruction of the world's natural resources, well, park-keeping is – well, very *important*.

Silence, then Anne sniggers softly. Liza is looking down at her plate.

ANNE (*whispering*) Boom boom.

RUSSELL Did I say anything?

BERENICE (*looking up, icily*) *Perhaps* we should all concentrate on eating. Couldn't we just?

Liza flicks a look at Paul, then everybody is eyes down to their plates.

12 The Hollanders' house

A small, dowdy terrace house. A battered moped draws up outside – it is Paul. He is nervous and tensed up as he dismounts and goes towards the house. He rings the doorbell. Mrs Maureen Hollander opens.

MAUREEN Yes?

PAUL Er, Mrs Hollander? I'm calling for my sister. Anne.

MAUREEN Oh. Anne. Oh, yes. Come in. Step inside.

13 The hall

MAUREEN (*calling upstairs*) Anne, it's your brother! – She's upstairs. With Liza. Anne! It's –

PAUL Paul!

ANNE What? Ah . . .

MAUREEN Ted! – (*to Paul*) You go in. Sit down. She won't be a . . .

14 The sitting-room

Ted is in his armchair, glued to the television.

MAUREEN Anne's brother. Come to – (*to Paul*) Nothing serious, I hope.

PAUL Serious?

MAUREEN I mean, wanting Anne.

PAUL Oh, no. Just calling for her.

Anne erupts into the room, Liza following.

ANNE (*annoyed*) I'm not late!

PAUL No. Thought I'd pick you up. Just for fun.

Anne stares for a moment, puzzled.

ANNE Well . . . you'll have to wait! Got to find my coat.

She goes, leaving Liza still watching Paul. The television is blaring. The three stand awkwardly, Ted's eyes are straying back to the screen.

MAUREEN Er – take your helmet off. Won't you?

PAUL (*eyes on Liza*) Yes.

MAUREEN (*to Ted – voice raised to penetrate TV noise*) It's Paul. Paul. Liza said he was keen on gardening.

TED Oh – ah – good.

LIZA (*louder*) No, I said he was talking about Dad's work.

PAUL Yes. They're the *lungs* of *London*, aren't they!

TED What are?

PAUL The parks! I mean the parks are! The lungs.

TED Oh.

MAUREEN Oh, turn the tele down, Ted! (*Doing so, agitated*) There. Now we can talk.

Silence. She looks from one to the other expectantly. But neither wants to talk, anyway.

PAUL Well, I . . .

TED Yer. Well.

Relief, as Anne bustles back into the room, buttoning up her coat. "Ah's" from the men, as Paul turns to Anne, Ted quickly back to his tele, putting the sound back up.

ANNE Where's the helmet then?

PAUL Here . . .

She snatches it and moves towards the hall.

MAUREEN Well, that was . . . see you again then . . . very interesting.

ANNE (*striding out*) Bye!

15 The hall

Paul, following, stops at the street door. Liza stops – so they are for this moment alone together, close. They whisper low, breathless, quick, confused.

PAUL I . . . well . . . nice –

LIZA Is it – is it *your* motorbike?

PAUL Yes – I – only a moped, really.
LIZA Must be fun.
PAUL Yes. You wouldn't...?
LIZA What?
PAUL Like a ride? Sometime?
LIZA Yer. Why not?
PAUL After school?

But Anne, helmeted, now barges back.

ANNE Here! Are you giving me a lift on that rotten moped or aren't you?
PAUL Yes. (*Grabs her exuberantly, to her astonishment, and pats her face*) Sure. Great.
ANNE (*to Liza, as she goes*) Crackers!

Liza grins ambiguously, a glint in her eye.

16 A park

Paul and Liza are wandering slowly among trees, helmets dangling from their hands, he not quite daring to touch her, her hand just evading his. He is talking loudly, excitedly – but his mind is probably not on what he is saying.

PAUL You see, trees! – without these trees we'd all suffocate. We'd all be dead.
LIZA Yer. Actually dead?
PAUL It's photosynthesis, you see.
LIZA Oh. It's biology is it?
PAUL Yes. Trees replace the oxygen we use up.
LIZA Good for trees!
PAUL We couldn't do without them. It's – it's symbiosis! We live in a symbiotic union!

She's close enough to grab, but he doesn't.

LIZA With trees?
PAUL And flowers!
LIZA (*grinning*) Flowers as well?
PAUL So it's true. The parks *are* the lungs.
LIZA My dad will be pleased!
PAUL Without these the world would be...
LIZA London would be...

PAUL (*nodding*) London, too.

LIZA (*sniffing deeply at a flower she has picked*) Ah! Without a breath of oxygen!

PAUL (*laughing*) No. It doesn't happen that . . . (*he takes her hand*) . . . that way.

LIZA (*trembling*) No?

PAUL (*trembling*) No . . . it's . . .

LIZA How . . . then . . .?

PAUL Liza.

LIZA Paul.

They kiss, slowly, the flower crushing between their two hands, then falling to the ground along with their helmets. We cut to a montage of still photos – Liza and Paul in the park, on the bike, meeting outside school, parting outside home, etc.

17 The Summers' sitting-room

Russell, seeing Paul's rucksack in the hall, enters the room. Anne is slumped on the sofa, discontented.

RUSSELL (*to Paul*) And where you off to this weekend?

PAUL Geology field trip, Dad.

RUSSELL *Again*? That's the second this month, isn't it?

PAUL Is it?

RUSSELL (*to Anne*) And what's the matter with you?

ANNE Oh. Nothing to do.

RUSSELL What about – what's her name – Liza?

ANNE Spending the weekend with her aunt! In the country!

RUSSELL I don't understand it. You were never in and he was never out. Now it's the complete reverse. What's happening? *Kids!*

18 A youth hostel

Paul and Liza are camping in the grounds. In a sequence of shots we see them wading through long grass, playing around on a rope walk, laughing and looking at one another across the flames of a camp fire. They are playing "Consequences" – Paul hands Liza a message.

LIZA (*unrolling the paper*) Saint Paul and Liza Minelli. Met on a desert island. They fell in love. He said, I think you're sweet. She said, I love you too. The world said "What a pleasant surprise!" And the consequence was – they lived happily ever after.

19 The snooker-room

Paul, obviously uneasy, is having a game with his father.

RUSSELL Four away again! What's the matter with you today? You're not concentrating. Are you!

PAUL No.

RUSSELL No fun playing with you if you don't concentrate.

He pockets a red ball.

PAUL Yes.

RUSSELL Without concentration . . . ah!

He pockets a black.

PAUL Dad. I've got to talk to you.

RUSSELL Um?

He sinks another red.

PAUL Dad . . .

RUSSELL (*lining up on the yellow*) Small fish are sweet.

PAUL (*blurting it out*) Dad, I'm going to get married.

RUSSELL (*irritated, not looking up*) Don't talk when I'm lining up a shot! (*Mistiming his shot*) *What* did you say?

PAUL I'm going to get married.

RUSSELL This a joke?

PAUL No.

RUSSELL Stop talking rubbish. Married to *whom*?

PAUL Liza.

RUSSELL Liza?

PAUL I've got to, Dad.

RUSSELL Liza? You mean – that – Anne's . . . You've got to?

PAUL Liza's going to have a baby.

20 The Hollanders' sitting-room

Maureen and Liza are leaning against each other in tears. There is an atmosphere of hysterics.

MAUREEN Oh, Liza. Oh, no. How could you? You wicked, stupid – Oh, you stupid – What will your father say! Behind our backs, too! Not a word! Why didn't you *take precautions*?

LIZA But Mum, you know how it is. You don't think it's going to happen!

MAUREEN Of course it'll happen! You stupid, silly...

LIZA Don't, oh Mum! It's all right. We're going to get married. We love each other!

21 The snooker-room

As before. Russell and Paul stand with the table between them.

RUSSELL (*furious*) Don't they teach you sex education at your school? You stupid *idiot*! "Didn't think it would happen"! You're thoroughly *irresponsible*! Do you hear me?

PAUL Yes. I'm not deaf.

RUSSELL (*raging on*) Did you think of *any*thing? Did you stop for one *moment* to consider...

PAUL But, Dad, you know how it is – in the excitement...

RUSSELL Like animals, you mean! *Animals*. Is that what you're saying?

PAUL No! We love each other! *That's* what I'm saying.

RUSSELL *I* love your mother. That doesn't mean I'm completely without control. *Normal* people take *precautions*!

PAUL All right! Perhaps you should have told me how, instead of leaving it to the bloody school! It might never have happened then.

RUSSELL Oh! Oh! So it's all my fault now! All *my fault!*

22 The Hollanders' sitting-room

They have both wept themselves slightly quieter.

LIZA (*pleading*) But it's no worse than you and Dad, is it?

MAUREEN How do you mean?

LIZA Well, you married because you were going to have *me*. It's just the same.

MAUREEN What a thing to come out with! Does that make it right? I didn't start when I was sixteen! No! I waited!

LIZA (*reduced to fresh tears, hugging her*) Oh! Mum, Mum! Don't, don't blame me!

MAUREEN (*weeping*) Oh, I don't, I don't blame you, darling, but why didn't you come to me? I could have made sure you were safe. Oh! I could have given you some of my pills.

LIZA But, Mum, we *are* going to get married.

MAUREEN (*quieter*) That's what he says now. How can you be sure?

LIZA (*passionate, convinced*) I *know*. *We are* getting married!

23 The snooker-room

The atmosphere is calmer, colder, deadlier.

PAUL I am. I *am*, Dad.

RUSSELL And how do you plan to support her? On your one pound a week pocket money?

PAUL I'll find work.

RUSSELL You'll leave school? Give up your A-levels?

PAUL Yes.

RUSSELL Your chance of a university?

PAUL Well . . . yes.

RUSSELL (*pausing*) You're not going to do it, you know. I'm not going to let you.

PAUL I am, Dad. I am.

24 The Hollanders' sitting-room

The storm is over. Maureen is gently cradling Liza in her arms.

MAUREEN There, there then . . . perhaps it'll all turn out all right, darling.

25 The snooker-room

RUSSELL (*murmuring grimly, not looking at Paul*) Your mother and I will never forgive you.

26 The park

Paul and Liza are lying close together on the grass, whispering.

LIZA Was it awful?

PAUL Pretty tough.

LIZA Did you mind?

PAUL No. They'll get used to it.

LIZA My Mum cried.

PAUL (*half laugh*) My Mum just went straight to bed. With a headache.

LIZA Your dad rang up and spoke to my dad.

PAUL Did he?

LIZA I think he arranged a meeting.

PAUL How do you mean?

LIZA Both families.

PAUL Where?

Silence.

LIZA They won't stop us, will they?

PAUL (*squeezing back*) Never.

Silence. They look at each other.

PAUL (*with feeling, defiant*) Let them just try and part us.

27 The Hollanders' sitting-room

The two families are gathered together: obvious tension in the air. They stand in a sort of circle.

RUSSELL (*giving a nod to Ted, a tight smile*) We brought Anne. Hope you don't mind. But, er, thought, to begin with at least, Anne could, er – the children could be together, while we – er have a preliminary discussion.

MAUREEN (*nervous*) Oh, yes. Sounds a good idea.

TED Oh, yer. True.

Liza and Paul are exchanging glances. She has stiffened, is ready to protest, but Paul is less sure of himself.

LIZA But . . .

MAUREEN Do you see, Liza?

LIZA (*ignoring Mum, looking at Russell, quite nervous*) Isn't this all about us?

All speak together

RUSSELL But of course.

TED Ah, now, Liza.

LIZA I think we ought to stay.

Russell senses things aren't quite going to plan.

RUSSELL Oh. Well, yes, certainly. No you're perfectly right. Anne, go back and wait in the car.

MAUREEN Oh, she could sit in the kitchen.

RUSSELL (*unwillingly*) Mmm, well. You be quiet then.

Anne fades unobtrusively into the kitchen but it is so small, and the door open, that she is practically in the room..

RUSSELL Right, now. Well, shall we all . . . be seated?

MAUREEN Yes . . . (*Smiling to Berenice, as they settle together on sofa*) Bit of a squash. (*Patting spare end of sofa*) Liza.

But Liza has moved towards Paul, and they sit together on a large chair near the kitchen door. Russell and Ted cannot decide where to sit.

RUSSELL Er . . .

TED No, you. Go on.

They sit.

MAUREEN (*nervously*) I did think of making a cup of tea!

RUSSELL Er, no. No, I don't think . . .

BERENICE No. No tea.

MAUREEN (*apologetic*) Oh, no, no . . .

RUSSELL Shall I begin? Paint the picture as we see it – Berenice and I? Then we can perhaps proceed from there.

MAUREEN Oh yes, that sounds . . . Eh, Liza?

RUSSELL Good. Now as we see it, there are two issues here. First of all we have two young people who feel very deeply for each other, who feel . . . to put it basically they are in love. Am I right so far?

There is silence.

TED (*clearing his throat*) Yes. But, of course, there's more . . .

RUSSELL Yes. And, of course, that's the second issue – this – this problem – which has – er – arisen.

TED Yes, er – (*nodding vaguely in the direction of Liza's stomach*) yes, that.

RUSSELL Now we would like to keep these two issues completely separate.

PAUL How can you?

RUSSELL Paul. Hear me out. Please. (*To Ted and Maureen*) Young people always seem to think we elders have no conception of how they feel. You, Paul. And Liza. I know. You're thinking here we all are, all of us old fogies sitting down to argue about something we know nothing about. But we were your age once. We've known what it is to be in love. Of course, we probably haven't faced exactly the same – problem – as you're faced with. (*Liza looks across to her mum*) But in many, many ways, our experience has been similar to yours. And we've learnt that it doesn't do to rush into things – without thought.

BERENICE (*coughing*) Yes, Russell.

RUSSELL Yes, so if we offer advice . . .

BERENICE Russell is trying to say that . . .

RUSSELL Yes, yes.

BERENICE We have no objection to the marriage, in itself.

RUSSELL Exactly!

BERENICE But we do think, *don't* we, Russell...

RUSSELL Yes, we think that this – this...

BERENICE (*harshly*) The pregnancy!

RUSSELL Yes! – should *not* be allowed to determine the – the whole issue.

BERENICE The marriage.

RUSSELL Right.

There is a short silence.

TED (*cautious*) Yes. But it has. Bound to.

RUSSELL Ah. Precisely. So we say is it fair? – is that fair to these young people? They are young, they're in love. They have a right to enjoy that youth, enjoy that love, to be given the chance to get to know each other thoroughly, in an unhurried way. I think we would all agree – surely – whatever a child is or is not, however wonderful, lovable, etcetera – it is a very heavy responsibility.

TED Oh, yes. It is that.

MAUREEN Oh yes, a baby.

RUSSELL For a young couple.

TED Oh, yes.

RUSSELL Is this the best way to embark upon a marriage?

TED No! (*Nodding to Liza*) He's right.

MAUREEN (*less confidently, upset*) Yes,... it makes for problems...

TED So... you're suggesting...?

RUSSELL There are alternatives.

TED Ah...

All eyes turn to Liza and Paul who sit still, troubled.

TED Well, I said to Maureen only last night didn't I?

MAUREEN But, well, we thought...

RUSSELL We are both thinking on the same lines?

TED (*with an uneasy flick of the eye at Liza*) Abort...

RUSSELL And there's also adoption.

TED Oh, yes. We hadn't really thought...

RUSSELL But, of course, the former...

BERENICE Much speedier.

They are all talking more quickly, more nervously, quieter.

RUSSELL Yes, would dispose – you know . . .

BERENICE Almost immediately.

TED But . . . is it that easy?

RUSSELL Oh, certainly. *Any* doctor – considering Liza's age.

BERENICE No problem.

MAUREEN (*secretly dismayed*) I never thought that . . .

RUSSELL (*relaxing now, cheerful*) And it's all managed very discreetly nowadays. Look, all we're saying *is* – (*to Ted and Maureen*) and we're speaking with complete frankness to each other, – we're saying aren't we – we're saying let's get this – this problem out of the way. If the children wish to marry then – all right. Bless them! Good enough! Or if perhaps they think it better to wait until, say, Paul gets his A-levels, perhaps goes to university – why, even better. (*Enthusiastically*) But they should be left to make up their own mind, in their own time! What we say is: destroy this element of *compulsion*!

LIZA (*quietly*) By destroying the baby.

MAUREEN Oh Liza . . .

RUSSELL No, Liza. Ah . . . (*Stops*) Now this, you see, was precisely *why* I wanted Liza to go off with Anne. Liza, quite rightly too, has an immediate emotional reaction to what I'm saying. This *is* an emotional subject to Liza. But, Liza, as parents, as the adults, we have to try to *look* at this in an *un*emotional way. Think what is the wisest course for your future.

TED Course. Course we do.

RUSSELL "Destroying a baby." We're not talking about a baby. Are we? We're talking about something almost invisible – an egg, an ovum, not *human*.

LIZA (*muttering*) Human to *me* . . .

RUSSELL Well, perhaps it's time we heard from your parents. Mr Hollander?

TED (*a little overwhelmed*) Well – er – Well, I think you've – you've about said it all.

MAUREEN You think then, Ted?

TED Yes, if . . . er –

RUSSELL (*smiling*) Russell.

TED Yes, if Russell thinks it can be arranged.

RUSSELL Oh. No question.

BERENICE Get a doctor's decision first thing tomorrow morning.

TED Well, then. Yes.

Silence. Liza looks silently at her father and mother but her face is frozen. Paul's face is uncertain, uneasy. Russell and Ted rise, smiling with a general sigh of relief.

RUSSELL I'm sure it's for the best... Ted.

TED (*grinning – man to man*) Least it settles the whole thing.

BERENICE Yes settled.

MAUREEN (*anxiously*) And Liza and Paul?

RUSSELL (*laughs*) Will have to be a little more careful in the future.

TED Control themselves. (*To Russell*) *We* 'ad to, didn't we?

RUSSELL Ah, yes. (*Laughs*) Indeed.

TED Don't want more frights like this.

By now the parents have got up to go and look altogether relieved. Then Maureen notices tears welling up inside Liza. Paul stands with a hand on her shoulder.

MAUREEN (*going to Liza*) There, there, pet. Nothing to cry about. It's all settled now.

LIZA (*suddenly*) It's *not* all settled!

The parents freeze in the doorway.

MAUREEN Shush. It isn't?

LIZA (*jumping up*) No! Because I'm not going to let them. They're not going to kill it!

TED Liza!

LIZA (*weeping*) I don't care! I don't care what you say! It's mine.

PAUL (*caught up in her excitement*) Yes, she's right, Dad!

ANNE (*hugging Liza from behind*) Good for you Liza!

The three kids are isolated. The adults stand nonplussed.

TED Now, look here, Liza.

RUSSELL (*mildly*) I thought I explained.

PAUL Stop getting at her, Dad! Liza knows what she wants!

RUSSELL And is this what you want, too?

Paul casts a glance at Liza, then Russell.

PAUL (*quietly*) Yes. We're having the baby. We're going on with the marriage.

RUSSELL (*thinly smiling to Ted*) It looks as if we all have to think again.

Part Two

28 The Summers' kitchen

Breakfast time. There is a distinct feeling of "the morning . . . after the night before." Russell is giving only half-hearted attention to the morning paper.

RUSSELL (*abruptly*) Did she say she was coming down?

ANNE Mum? – poor woman. In *her* condition?

RUSSELL You took her up the aspirin?

ANNE (*nodding*) Mm.

Russell dips his head again into the paper.

ANNE Hitting the old grapejuice were you then last night?

RUSSELL What's *that* supposed to mean?

ANNE Don't you know?

RUSSELL (*icily*) Your mother and I, yes, we *did* have a few, a few drinks. After yesterday's *performance* we felt we deserved it!

He buries his head in the paper.

ANNE (*innocently*) Oh, yes. It *was* a good performance you put on.

RUSSELL (*bursting up from the paper, ferociously*) I meant – Pah!

ANNE (*dreamily, twisting the knife in the wound*) Fancy. I'll be an aunt, won't I . . . Isn't it exciting? Do you know, Paul?

PAUL What?

ANNE All our class have already started knitting. For the baby! A complete outfit. We've got permission. Going to make it in Needlework class.

RUSSELL My God. Is that the truth? The school agreed to . . .

ANNE (*rising to go*) Why ever not?

RUSSELL It's a wonder they haven't elected Liza school captain . . .!

ANNE Oh, poor old Dad! You're taking all this too tragically you know. (*Flinging an arm around him, whispering deafeningly into one ear*) Didn't anyone ever tell you? God believes in happy endings!

She skips off out into the hall.

ANNE See you, honeys!

The street door slams behind her. Paul and Russell are left alone – Paul begins hurriedly doing up his briefcase and rises to leave.

RUSSELL You . . . don't have to go for a moment, do you?

PAUL (*awkward*) Well, don't want to be late.

RUSSELL You're leaving at the end of term! Being late for one morning . . . (*breaks off*). Oh, I'm sorry!

PAUL Quite all right.

RUSSELL But I *would* like to talk with you.

PAUL Really, not now Dad, it won't do any good you know.

RUSSELL I promise you I won't say a word against Liza! I just want to talk!

PAUL But . . . you'll be late.

RUSSELL I will *not* be late. Even if I were . . . (*His temper snapping, he jumps up*) Oh, for God's sake, will you sit down!

Both resume their seats.

RUSSELL Listen! Try to forget it's me talking to you. Will you? Just imagine – try! – that I'm a complete stranger! I realise every word I say to you is discounted because I'm your *father*, I'm the *enemy*.

PAUL That's not true!

RUSSELL There's a barrier between us! Don't try to say there isn't! And all right, it's my fault. If we'd been closer this might never . . .

PAUL It *would* have happened, Dad. I'm old enough to know my own mind.

RUSSELL Are you? You're four years younger than I was when I first married! *I* wasn't old enough to know my own mind!

PAUL People grow up earlier these days.

RUSSELL Oh, *that* old rubbish! (*Pause*) I'm sorry.

Silence. Then he begins talking hurriedly in an altered voice, almost timidly.

RUSSELL It's *because* it has happened to me, because I mucked up one marriage, and – I can remember how I felt – *you* know, before – how *sure* I was – you understand what I'm trying to say? (*appealing*) Paul, I'm not out to kid you. Love is a kind of . . . chemical reaction between people. Anyone will tell you this. A kind of . . . *infection*. You catch it. And, I woke up one day – after a year or so – to find I'd married someone with whom I – I shared nothing, no identity of interests – you know what I mean? Someone I didn't even like. You see, we hadn't taken the time – before marriage – to find out whether we were really suited to each other. You see? Paul . . . you understand?

There is silence from Paul.

RUSSELL So when I look at you now, how can I *not* envisage the possibility of this same situation recurring – you, one year from now, wondering why, why? And if it does come to that, think – how are you going to feel about the opportunities you are letting slip – school, university, our plans for your future? A year from now. When it's too late.

A pause.

PAUL But it won't come to that.

RUSSELL How can you be sure? You can't be sure! Listen. Think of the trouble it would have saved *me* – the argument, the heart-break – if I'd only waited those few years until I met Mummy.

PAUL (*grinning*) And made the perfect marriage.

RUSSELL (*stiffening*) We're not discussing Mummy and me. No marriage is perfect, but . . . Oh, all right! If you *won't* listen!

PAUL For God's sake, Dad, I'm not marrying Liza just to annoy you. (*Shouting*) I'm doing it because I have to!

RUSSELL But that's it. You don't have to! Liza could easily bring up the child by herself!

PAUL (*revolted*) Oh, no! You're asking me to run out on her?

RUSSELL Not that! *We'd* pay for everything, there'd be no hardship for her, Paul, I promise.

PAUL I'm marrying her! Get that in your head! It's settled!

Paul jumps up and makes for the door. Russell stands in front of him.

RUSSELL You have no conception of the problems you will face!

PAUL (*quietly*) No. All right, Dad. Out of my way.

Paul pushes past him into the hall, and Russell follows.

RUSSELL You're so innocent! It makes me want to weep.

PAUL (*politely*) Feel free, Dad.

RUSSELL You have nowhere to live. You have no job! And yet you can lightheartedly say it's all sett . . .

PAUL We're going to deal with all that, Dad. We're not totally brainless. In fact – let me surprise you, Dad – I'm going for a job tomorrow, as it happens!

RUSSELL A job? Where?

PAUL A job in the parks. Liza's dad has got me an interview. You see, Dad?

RUSSELL A job in the parks! You don't know one bloody end of a plant from the other!

29 The park

It is a dull, dreary day. Paul and Liza, looking a little lost and uncertain, are trying to attract the attention of a man driving a mechanical mower. Paul's efforts are unconvincing, rather pathetic.

PAUL (*running a few steps, shouting*) Excuse me – excuse me – Mr Arbuthnot? – Arbuthnot?

The man looks but continues mowing.

LIZA Shout louder!
PAUL Excuse me – could you – pardon me.

The machine sweeps on. Paul is exasperated.

PAUL (*to Liza*) The only way I'll stop him is to lie down in front of the machine!
LIZA Let me try. What's his name? A . . .
PAUL Arbuthnot.

Liza rushes at the machine, determined, forceful, much more positive than Paul. She shouts commandingly.

LIZA Mister! Stop! Stop!

The man, startled, stops almost immediately, leaving the engine running.

LIZA We want to see Mr Arbuthnot.
KEEPER Arbuthnot.
LIZA The Park Superintendent.
KEEPER Oh, him. In those huts. You see there. (*Pointing*) Huts. His office is over there.
LIZA Thanks very much.

The two walk towards the huts. They confront the Park Superintendent's door and knock.

LIZA (*whispering encouragingly*) You know what to say.
PAUL I suppose so.
LIZA Will I come in with you?
PAUL No, I'm all right. No . . .

Paul is startled by a shout from within: "Come." He pushes quickly into the hut.

30 Inside the hut

A bare, undecorated interior. Arbuthnot is a burly, brutal-looking man – he looks up irritably at Paul.

BUTHNOT I've said "come in" twice already.

PAUL I'm sorry. Didn't hear you.

BUTHNOT (*staring*) Mm. Has it started yet?

PAUL What?

BUTHNOT The rain.

PAUL Oh. Oh, no. I don't think so.

BUTHNOT It will. Well?

PAUL Er. What?

BUTHNOT (*irritated*) What do you want to see me about?

PAUL Ah. I'm Paul Summers. Mr Hollander. He said he'd spoken to you. About me.

BUTHNOT Ah. Yer. (*Eyeing the school uniform*) But you're still at school. Are you?

PAUL Leaving at the end of term.

BUTHNOT Ah. Well, er. And you think you'd *take* to this kind of work, do you?

PAUL Oh, yes. Yes, I *would* like it.

BUTHNOT Fancy working out in this? Eh? This is what you're faced with. More often than not.

The sound of rain is heard.

PAUL Yes. Oh, I don't mind.

BUTHNOT No? Bit of a bloody idiot if you don't. Aren't you?

PAUL No. But I'm – oh, I'm very keen, Mr – er . . . Arbuthnot. If you'll . . . just give me a chance.

BUTHNOT Um . . . Well, we'll have to think it over. Not even certain we'll have a vacancy yet. I'll let Ted know.

He resumes writing. Paul is not quite sure whether he has been dismissed.

PAUL Er.

BUTHNOT (*looks up*) That's all right, then. (*Starts writing again*) Don't get wet, will yer.

Paul exits.

31 Outside the hut

Liza is sheltering from the rain under the eaves.

LIZA (*eager*) How was it?
PAUL (*depressed*) Oh, all right.
LIZA It *was*? Sure?
PAUL Yer. Course. Great. (*Laughs*) Now we can start looking for a flat, can't we?

They look out of the curtain of rain, laugh, turn, up their collars, link arms and run. Paul's high spirits are not convincing.

32 A sequence of camera shots

Paul and Liza are seen searching through various notice boards. "No children, no pets" meets their eyes with almost every advert. We watch them with people on doorsteps shaking heads, offering depressing refusals.
They grow more and more weary, gamely trying to keep smiling, each to cheer the other.

33 The Summers' house: kitchen

Paul, Anne, Russell and Berenice are having tea. There is an oppressive silence, but Paul is tensing himself to speak.

PAUL Dad . . . Mum . . . (*Silence*).
RUSSELL (*looking up after a moment*) What? Come on. I'm not a thought reader.
PAUL Liza and me . . . we've been looking for a flat, you know, Dad.
RUSSELL (*ironical*) And you've found one, of course.
PAUL No.
RUSSELL You won't. Not round here. I have warned you, haven't I.
PAUL All right, Dad, I'm not asking for a sermon.
RUSSELL Mmm. Well, what *are* you asking? What do you want?
PAUL Doesn't matter now.
ANNE They could both come . . .
RUSSELL You keep out of this. (*To Paul*) What about her house? Isn't there room for you there?
PAUL Of course there isn't! – not for the two of us anyway.
RUSSELL (*laughing*) *Three* of us.
PAUL (*angry*) *Yes*. Right! Oh forget it Dad. I'm sorry I spoke.
RUSSELL No. *You* brought the subject up, Paul.
PAUL Well, I'm saying I'm sorry I did. I'm saying forget it.
RUSSELL But I'm not going to, Paul.
BERENICE (*suddenly erupting*) Oh, for God's sake! You heard him! Drop the damn subject.

There is a slight pause, all three taken aback by her furious intervention.

RUSSELL Well, darling. They've got to find *somewhere* to live.

BERENICE I'm sick to *death* of hearing about them. And their *stupid* affair!

RUSSELL But – but he's still our son, isn't he? We still have a duty.

BERENICE (*viciously*) No. *You* have a duty! If you want to think so. And you can get on with doing your duty. But count me out!

RUSSELL Berenice . . .

BERENICE Don't 'Berenice' me. I'm not one of your bloody snotty-nosed students!

RUSSELL This is a ridiculous attitude!

BERENICE (*screaming*) He got himself into this mess! Let him get on with it. I've washed my hands of it! It's a fine bloody state of affairs – isn't it! – when we can't even have our tea in peace – we – Ooh! (*getting to her feet*).

RUSSELL But – darling . . .

She turns and runs out, the door slamming behind her. Russell makes to follow, then subsides back in his chair. The two children look appalled.

34 Paul's room

Paul is lying on his back, rather as he was in the first scenes of the play. But now there are no exercise books open – he is not working, but listening to a discussion programme on the radio. The subject is marriage – the programme finishes with a rendering of "Love and marriage go together like a horse and carriage". We watch Paul listening, depressed, frowning, moody . . .

35 The Summers' house: hallway

The bell shrills out and Paul opens the front door to Liza. They exchange a very quick kiss, Liza glaring at the kitchen and sitting-room doors. Paul is looking happier, more relaxed.

PAUL It's all right. They're both out.

She opens her mouth in a relieved, mischievous grin.

PAUL I haven't moved anything yet.

LIZA No, good.

PAUL Well, they only decided last night you see. Talking all bloody evening.

They scamper upstairs.

36 The snooker-room

They stand, hand-in-hand in the doorway.

PAUL What do you think?

LIZA Yer . . . oh, yer.

PAUL With my room, you see, as the kitchen.

LIZA Yer.

PAUL My dad says it would be easy to get some water run in there from downstairs. We could have an electric stove. *And* a fridge. There's a wallplug . . .

LIZA Yer. Great.

PAUL Course we might need a power point but . . .

LIZA (*decided*) It'll be fab . . .

They embrace. After a moment, she whispers.

LIZA I forgot, I've got good news for you, too.

PAUL Yer?

LIZA That job – you know? My dad says you've got it!

PAUL (*with mixed feelings*) Ah. Well, that's . . .

LIZA Great.

PAUL Yer!

LIZA Things are really working out. They are! Aren't they!

PAUL Tremendous. Everything's – ah – yer.

He breaks away and crosses to the table.

LIZA We'll have to get rid of this.

PAUL We'll stick it in the basement.

LIZA Perhaps it'd do for our bed!

PAUL My Dad' would have a fit! (*Laughing, imitating Russell*) "Ruin the surface." "Not levelled up."

LIZA (*laughing*) Remember that first time?

PAUL When you fell off?

LIZA It all started here. Didn't it?

PAUL Falling?

LIZA Falling for *you*.

PAUL (*reflective, as they face each other over the table*) Yer . . .

LIZA (*tenderly*) You were funny. You know I said to Anne afterwards, why does he always talk as if he's got a frog in his throat.

PAUL (*grinning*) Only with *you*.

LIZA (*laughing*) The way you went on about my Dad.

PAUL I didn't know what I was saying. (*Giggling*) Lungs of London!

LIZA If it hadn't been for that stupid school gymnastics I would never...

PAUL (*less bright*) We would never have met.

LIZA No. And now look – (*holding her stomach*) I'm out of the gymnastics. I'm out of the school...(*Sensing Paul's unease*) Funny... how things... happen.

PAUL Yes.

LIZA You're...

PAUL What?

LIZA Paul you're not sorry, are you?

PAUL Course I'm not. Why should you say that?

LIZA We've got everything we want now. The job won't be too bad. You'll like it, I'm sure you will.

PAUL Yer. Course.

Silence. She looks at him.

PAUL *Course.*

LIZA You... You could carry on studying at nightschool. Couldn't you? I mean, if...

PAUL (*turning away*) I don't want to carry on studying. Load of rubbish, the whole of it. (*Changing the subject to cover his disquiet*) I reckon we should have the bed over here. Eh? Do you reckon? We don't want to be under the window, because of the draughts. Some terrible draughts in this room...

His voice dies away. Liza is looking at him, stunned, gradually realising.

PAUL Will we? I mean, will we? Or should we, er...

LIZA (*quiet*) I think you *are* sorry.

PAUL I am *not*.

LIZA Do you think I should have had an abortion?

PAUL No of course not! Who said *that*? I stood up for you then! I supported you!

LIZA Then? Then? What about *now*?

PAUL *Now*? I do *now*? (*Angrily*) So shut up! Stupid talk! We're discussing where to put the bed, aren't we?

She starts crying – Paul goes over to cuddle her.

PAUL Oh for God's sake... Liza... Oh don't... I haven't *said* anything, I didn't say...Anyway, what's the *use* of all this arguing? We've got to get on with it! We can't change anything now!

LIZA (*looking up at him, slowly*) But we can.

PAUL How? Get an abortion? (*Pause*) *What* then? What are you talking about?

She still doesn't answer. Silence. A bang on the door and Anne enters hugging a portable television.

ANNE (*excited*) Hello, fans! What do you think? Just remembered this. We hardly ever use it. The very thing for rearing healthy babies. Got to ask you – we're in a real desperate state – the class! – with all this *knitting*. We keep missing out button holes and arms, and legs and things! So we've decided we're going to give all the knitting to War on Want and collect for a wedding present instead. What...? (*She falters.*)

The atmosphere has got through to her.

LIZA (*quietly in control*) You needn't bother. There isn't going to be a wedding.

ANNE *Not*?

PAUL Liza!

LIZA (*to Paul*) No. I'm going to bring up the baby by myself.

ANNE Liza! Don't...

LIZA (*tearful again*) Yes, I can live at my mum's. Don't you worry. (*Choking*) It's all going to work out for the best – it will! It will – it will...

She runs out leaving Paul and Anne stunned.

PAUL (*calling feebly*) Liza!

ANNE (*thrusting him forward*) Run *after* her! Go on! Don't just stand there!

Then aghast, as she looks at him. Paul moves away, guiltily.

ANNE You're *pleased*... *pleased*. (*Slowly whispering*) You bloody *coward*! You've let them frighten you out of it. Haven't you?

37 The hallway

Paul walks, head down, towards the stairs and descends. Liza stands below.

LIZA You'll be sorry for this, Paul. You wait. You'll be sorry.

38 A montage of stills and film

Liza running in the street, tears streaming. Paul in school uniform, pens in pockets, satchel on back, driving along on moped, face expressionless. Liza entering a Maternity Welfare Clinic. Paul at a school desk – far too small for him – working in an exercise book. Large hospital ward, narrowing down on Liza in bed. Baby, smiling. Huge examination room, narrowing down on Paul, working, pale concentrated. Liza pushing small pram, smiling over it, entering a shop. Paul, college scarf, etc. climbing steps into university building. Older. Grown a beard. University bar, Paul drinking with friends – winking at barmaid.

FRIEND *You* married?

PAUL (*laughing*) Not me. I'm too young to die.

39 A London park

Paul and Liza are sitting on a secluded bench, a nervous foot or two apart. They are older, and look it. Liza looks more sophisticated and much more at ease than Paul, who appears vulnerable and hesitant. Beside the bench is Paul's motorbike, a larger and smarter vehicle than his old moped. We enter at what is a pause near the beginning of a quiet but slightly awkward conversation.

LIZA (*nodding to motorbike*) Better than your old one.

PAUL Yes.

LIZA What happened to that?

PAUL Oh ... just wore out. Anne had it for a while.

LIZA How *is* Anne?

PAUL She's all right. You don't see her now?

Liza smiles and shakes her head.

PAUL She's at South London Poly. She's doing all right.

LIZA And you?

PAUL Oh, yer. Great. It's great down at Bristol. Hard work, but – (*Then blurting out, almost angry*) Why didn't you ...?

LIZA What?

PAUL Well – you haven't brought ...

LIZA Suzy? It's awkward bringing her on a bus. I didn't know you'd want to see her.

PAUL My own kid?

LIZA Well ... You haven't bothered too much these last three years.

PAUL I have.

LIZA We could have met at the house if you *really* wanted to see her.

PAUL I feel bad about going to your parents' house. You *know* that.

LIZA But that's stupid!

Silence.

PAUL Anyway . . . I thought we could talk easier . . . like this.

LIZA What about?

PAUL My Dad's written to me. He says you won't take any more money . . . He says you returned the last lot of money. The money for Suzy.

LIZA Yes. That's right.

PAUL But why?

LIZA I don't need it.

PAUL But *Suzy* needs it!

LIZA She doesn't. Not any longer. I'm working now. I earn good money. I can look after her by myself.

PAUL That's ridiculous! My dad can spare it!

LIZA (*smiling*) I'm *sure* he can. That doesn't matter.

PAUL (*bewildered*) Does this mean you're never going to take any more money? What about when – when I start earning? Will you refuse to take money from *me*?

LIZA (*cheerfully*) Probably.

PAUL But – I – she's *my* child as much as *yours*. You'll just have to take the money!

LIZA (*laughing*) You'll *force* me?

PAUL No, but –

LIZA You think I'll hide Suzy away from you?

PAUL (*angrily*) A child *needs* a father!

LIZA (*growing angry herself*) All right! You're *still* her father. You can always *see* her. Whenever you want! But you can't expect me to bring her up under orders from *your dad*, kept by *your dad*! I just can't take that – the feeling that we're under obligation to him the whole bloody time! She's *my* responsibility now. Mine, Paul!

PAUL Yer, but – one parent families! They're not *enough*! Everybody says so!

LIZA Oh, well.

PAUL Wh – what do you mean, oh well?

LIZA (*slight pause*) We may not be a one parent family for much longer.

Silence. He stares at her.

PAUL You have a boy-friend?

LIZA Yer...

PAUL Marrying him? You're marrying him?

LIZA Maybe. Ah, don't worry. He *loves* Suzy. He does. Really. Ah, come on Paul. He does. He plays with her, he looks after her. For Christ's sake, he's done more for her than you've ever done.

PAUL It's not that.

LIZA Then what?

PAUL I suppose... (*nervously*) I don't like to think I'm... losing you.

Silence. Now it is her turn to stare.

LIZA Oh, Paul... We lost each other three years ago, didn't we?

PAUL I didn't think so.

LIZA If we had married, if we'd stuck together, things would be different. But... oh, Paul, we're not the same people we were then. Are we? I mean – the world doesn't stand still while you go off to your university. Can't you see? If you have any feelings about me – now – why that's in your head! It's a – a kind of silly dream, it's three years out of date! Isn't it? Honestly? Honestly, Paul?

PAUL (*painful*) Couldn't we... We could try again.

LIZA What with?

PAUL (*almost in tears*) But we had something. We did love each other. I *did* love you. And if I – well, you know – if I...

LIZA Yer. I know.

PAUL (*crying out*) I couldn't *help* it at the time!

LIZA (*tenderly, almost crying herself*) Yes. yes. Oh, Paul. And I was mad about *you*. I was. But we can't change it now. Ah, don't. It's not worth getting upset about. (*Smiles*) Poor Saint Paul.

PAUL (*whispers, grinning*) And Liza Minelli...

The camera draws back until they are small, isolated figures sitting on their bench. Campside flames leak into the screen. We hear Liza's voice, continuing.

LIZA Met on a desert island
They fell in love
He said, I think you're sweet,
She said, I love you too
The world said, what a pleasant surprise
And the consequence was...

Points for Discussion and Suggestions for Writing

(Suggestions for writing are marked with an asterisk.)

Coins Against the Wall

1 In what ways are we made aware of the uneasy relationship between David and his father during the first scene and throughout the play? What examples are there of David being mentally bullied by his father? Try to sum up in your own words the sort of person you imagine Harry Briars to be.

2 Mr Matthews tells David that "Some mothers might not care too much, but your mother most certainly does" (Scene 17). What signs are there that Mrs Briars is over-protective towards her son? Do you feel that she is in any way responsible for David being the victim of bullies?

3 Do you think the teacher treats David sympathetically in scenes 3 and 4? Think about any occasion when you had a similar encounter with a teacher – was he or she understanding and sympathetic. Is it possible to confide in teachers over certain problems?

4 What impression do you have of Jimmy and Singet Rey? Are there any indications in the play that they guess what is going on from the beginning?

*5 What is your reaction to Mick's comment that he and Arthur are "deprived of parental affection" (Scene 8)? Write the scene between Mick and his parents when they discover he has been extorting money from another boy.

6 How does the playwright highlight David's isolation from everyone around him? If you were directing the play for television which particular moments would you focus on to reveal his loneliness? Do you feel any sympathy for David or has he himself to blame? What is your attitude to "loners" you know at school?

*7 David ends up stealing from his mother. Discuss the rights and wrongs of "borrowing" from friends or parents. Write a scene, as a play or story, in which you are "caught in the act"; it can be serious or amusing.

8 Mrs Briars tells David: "Your father would like you to be..." (Scene 1). Discuss what she might have gone on to say. Is it still true today that parents expect their sons to behave differently from their daughters? What do you think your attitude will be towards your own children in the future?

9 David asks if he can change schools to avoid the bullying. What would you do in Mrs Briars' position?

10 The Headmaster comments: "Isn't it strange that we say *playing* truant about something so serious?" (Scene 17). There are many different dialect words and phrases meaning "to truant"; find out about them and their origins.

11 Mr Matthews also declares: "School used to be like medicine: it did you good, so it didn't matter if you didn't like the taste" (Scene 17). How do you think he feels schools have changed – and have they? What is meant by child-centred education? Discuss your own school's ethos or philosophy. How would you like to see it change?

*12 Comment on the Headmaster's treatment of the bullying incidents. What does the writer suggest in the stage direction – "Silence is maintained for two seconds" (Scene 18)? Can you think of a similar scene at your own school: how did pupils react? Write an account of events in the classroom after Mr Matthews' exit.

*13 "Every school has its Arthurs and its Micks." Use this as a starting point for a story.

14 "Bullies are blusterers, cowards, tyrants" (Scene 18) observes Mr Matthews. Debate this statement with reference to our own and other societies.

15 Improvise a short drama based on the game Coins Against the Wall.

*16 Improvise or write the scene in which Jimmy and Singet Rey work out a plan to defeat Mick and Arthur. Compose a story in which the bullies of the plot are justly punished.

*17 Continue the story, in narrative or play form, of David's next few days at school... or playing truant.

The Kids Are Okay

18 Look carefully at the stage directions in the opening scenes. How important are they in establishing the setting

and creating the right kind of atmosphere? If you were directing the play how would you emphasise this background?

19 What devices are employed by the writer in the first part of the play to create a sense of tension between Andrew and Mary? Andrew says: "It's just the little things that build up until it... until there's nothing left" (Scene 16). What seem to be the main sources of contention between the parents? Do you sympathise with or blame either side?

20 Why do you think Jill is always turning to her toy animals? What do they represent for her? Think about how you would bring out the significance of the animals if you were directing the play. You may also like to find out about a famous play *The Glass Menagerie* by American playwright Tennessee Williams, in which a collection of glass animals plays a similar role.

21 "There's nothing clean to wear. No shirts. Mum's not bothering," (Scene 7) complains Kenny. What is your reaction to Kenny's words and to his expecting Jill to do the washing? Could Jill and Kenny have done anything to prevent their parents separating? Act out a short scene in which the two of them discuss ways of helping their mother and father stay together.

*22 There are several classroom scenes in the play: what do they contribute to the overall effect of the drama? Write a brief character sketch of Mr Mulveen based on what we see of him with Kenny.

23 Think in detail about the actual structure of the play and its division into two parts. In what ways do the scenes offer balance and development in dramatic terms? What are we led to expect from the titles *The Kids Are Okay, Who's Leaving*? and *Father's Day*? Can you think up more appropriate or interesting titles?

*23 What is the writer trying to show us by beginning Part Two with Mary talking to Mr Mulveen? How do Andrew and Mary differ in their approach to their son's education? Devise a short script in which Andrew and David are arguing the advantages and disadvantages of staying on at school.

25 Improvise the scene at the house when Andrew arrives to take the children out for their Sunday treat. How do you

imagine the children to be feeling? Try to bring out the unspoken tensions and unhappiness that Mary must be feeling. What sort of mood is Andrew in?

*26 Discuss the children's changing attitudes towards Doreen during their trip to Loch Lomond. What is your impression of Doreen from what she says and how she responds to Andrew and the children? Try to sum up in your own words how she feels; then imagine what she might have written as her diary entry for that day when she arrived home. This can be set out as a series of notes – or cartoons!

27 At which points in the play does it seem that Kenny and Jill are caught in the cross-fire between adults? Search through the script to see where this happens – in scene 30 for example. How might you have reacted in similar circumstances? What does Gran's presence add to the drama?

28 Andrew confides in Doreen: "As long as I can keep friends with the kids, see them right. I talk more to them once a week than I did when I was living with them" (Scene 34). Why might this be true? Bearing in mind what he says to Mary in scene 39, what are your feelings towards Andrew at this stage in the play?

29 What indications are there that Doreen sees no permanence in her relationship with Andrew? What are his feelings on the subject?

*30 Doreen and Mary meet briefly in the club bar. Imagine they meet together by themselves on another occasion some weeks later, perhaps after Jill's stay in hospital. Write the scene that takes place.

31 Do you find Jill's overdose attempt credible? How are we prepared for it in the preceding scenes? Jill obviously works herself into a certain frame of mind before swallowing the pills. If you were taking her part in the play how would you act the role?

32 Suicide is still the fourth most common cause of death in this country. Each year about 4000 people deliberately kill themselves and about ten times as many make unsuccessful attempts to "put an end to it all". Discuss some of the issues that might lie behind suicide and find out about the Samaritans organisation. You might extend your debate to the question of euthanasia and the orga-

nisation called EXIT.

*33 It is often difficult to bring a play to a satisfying conclusion. In fact Jack Ronder wrote an alternative ending. Are you happy with the way the play ends? Is the writer trying to show that lessons have or have not been learned? Make up your own concluding sequence to the drama.

*34 Take any of the following as starting points for a short story:
"The Kids Are Okay."
"She's blaming him. He's blaming her."
"People do get bogged down, with the best intentions."

If Only

35 Do you find the opening sequence of camera shots convincing as they are set out in the stage directions? Discuss how they might be presented if you were acting the play on stage or in the classroom. Look in detail at the use of the "voice over" technique throughout the play; what in dramatic terms are its advantages and disadvantages?

36 Is your enjoyment of the play in any way spoiled because you know from the outset how the plot develops? Are the flashbacks (asterisked in the text) an effective dramatic device? Think about other plays or films you have seen in which flashback scenes were an important feature: what difficulties do you imagine they presented to the director?

37 Micky asks Brian: "We've got sixty more years at the very least. What are you going to do with all those hours?" (Scenes 2 and 3). Do you ever ask yourself the same question? What conclusions do you come to?

38 What seem to be the main reactions from Brian's family to his grief over Micky's death?

*39 "There are two kinds of people in this world, Bri, those who do things, and those who just think about doing them" (Scene 7). How is this not altogether serious comment from Micky significant to the action of the play? Try dividing up your own family and friends in this way – is it a useful generalisation? Write a short story with this sentence as either a starting or finishing point.

40 In scene 9 why does Brian's father think about tearing up the photograph and then decide not to?

*41 What impression do you form of Doctor West? What does he think is actually wrong with Brian? Make up an interview between a doctor and patient in which they are talking at cross-purposes; it could be serious or amusing.

*42 "First thing on the list when I make my packet..." (Scene 18). Micky says it will be a house with a garden for his mum. What would yours be? Write a story about your fantasy spending spree.

*43 Why does Brian break into the school? Write a story or poem about your school at night. You might also like to read Willy Russell's excellent and disturbing play *Break In* published in "*Scene* Scripts Two" (Longman Imprint) where stealing into a school gets completely out of hand.

44 Mrs Thompson's long speech at the end of *If Only* is a powerful piece of drama. What is the central reason why she does not want Brian in her home? How does Mary react towards Brian? What are your feelings towards him at this point and throughout the play?

45 The stereo headphones are a recurrent image here rather like Jill's toy animals in *The Kids Are Okay*. What are they a symbol of for Brian?

*46 Micky's "voice over" is an important part of the play and needs to be convincing. If you were the director what sort of tone, pitch or accent would you give him? How do you visualise Micky as a teenager – does he seem naturally happy or sad? Look closely at the text and then write a character description of him.

47 "He's in mourning for Micky. Stricken with grief. Takes people in funny ways" (Scene 5). Do you consider Brian's behaviour realistic? Discuss examples of people you know or have heard about whose lives have been deeply affected by death and subsequent grief.

*48 Piece together the events leading up to and including Micky's drowning and write them as a short story. The narrative could be told from Brian's viewpoint or that of a passerby. *Or* devise the story as it might appear in the local newspaper the following day.

49 If you look back over the play you will discover that its structure involves an intricate threading together of many short scenes. Comment on the success or otherwise of

this. David Cook, the playwright, also puts a lot of humour into the play: is this an effective way of tackling such a serious subject as death? Do you feel that there are certain topics which should not be treated lightly? Discuss the way in which television's situation comedy programmes address themselves to serious issues in our society?

Consequences

50 Russell shouts at his son Paul in the second part of the play: "There's a barrier between us! Don't try to say there isn't!" (Scene 28). In what ways do we sense the traditional conflict between parents and their teenage children during the opening scenes? Is the "Generation Gap" inevitable? Give reasons for your opinions.

51 Describe how the writer sets up the first of the "consequences" early on in the play. Then go through the whole text carefully to discover how Leonard Kingston structures the plot around a series of dramatic "consequences".

*52 Write a character sketch of each member of the Summers household, concentrating on those aspects which you think are most likely to bring them into conflict with one another. Build up your description both from what the characters say and from what the playwright tells you about them.

53 Contrast the Summers' and Hollanders' households. In what ways and why are they presented as being very different?

*54 Looking at his speech and the stage directions in scene 19, discuss how Paul is shown to be nervous. Imagine yourself in his position (or in Liza's in the following scene). How might you approach the subject with your mother or father? Write out the conversation that takes place, and include plenty of directions as to the mood and feelings of the speakers.

55 Think about how the scenes (19–25) involving Liza and Maureen, and Paul and Russell, are linked together and skilfully orchestrated. What seems to you particularly realistic or unrealistic about those scenes?

56 To what extent do both Paul and Liza make their parents

feel a sense of guilt over what has happened? Do you feel either parent could be held in any way responsible?

*57 When the two families hold their "summit meeting", the natural tensions between them are cleverly exploited. Discuss how the playwright does this. Why do you think Russell Summers takes the lead in the proceedings even though the scene takes place at the Hollanders' home. Write a short dramatic piece in which your own parents meet up with someone else's to discuss a delicate matter.

58 "Young people always seem to think we have no conception of how they feel. You, Paul. And Liza. I know. You're thinking here we all are, all of us old fogies sitting down to argue about something we know nothing about" (Scene 27). What do you imagine Paul and Liza are thinking at this point? Do you feel Russell is sensible or insensitive in his whole approach? Think about the last occasion your mother or father lectured you about something. What were your inner thoughts at the time, and what did you actually say?

59 "I think we would all agree, whatever a child is or is not – it is a very heavy responsibility" (Scene 27). Have Paul and Liza thought about this enough? Would you say that many people – particularly those who marry young – have children without considering this "heavy responsibility"?

60 "We're talking about something almost invisible – an egg, an ovum, not *human*" (Scene 27). Do you agree with Russell's observation? Abortion is a subject that frequently causes heated debate – what are your views? Debate the relative merits of abortion and adoption from the mother's or father's point of view.

61 What, would you guess, triggers Liza's decision to keep the baby? Might she have reacted differently if the parents had been less assertive?

*62 "Oh, poor old dad! You're taking all this too tragically" (Scene 28). Why does Anne deliberately taunt and provoke her father at the start of Part Two? Can you think of an occasion when you have done this to another member of your family? Write about it, as a story or poem, and about any regrets you may have felt afterwards.

63 Russell reveals in scene 28 that he has been married once before. Contrast what he has to say about marriages and

their failure with what Andrew has to say in *The Kids Are Okay* (Scene 16). Reading back through the play, at which point do you sense that Paul decides not to go through with the marriage?

64 What is it that prompts Berenice's outburst in scene 33? Are you surprised by her reaction and what are your feelings towards her?

65 Why, in scene 36, does Liza finally decide to go it alone? Would you have sided with Anne's concluding comments, or do you consider their separation to be the right solution for both of them?

*66 Write the letter Paul must have sent to Liza asking her to meet up with him. Imagine the mood he might have been in at the time of drafting the note.

67 Try to sum up Paul's and Liza's inner feelings when they meet again after a long time apart. Paul says: "One parent families! They're not *enough*!" (Scene 39). Is he right? Why does Liza not want Paul's support in the future? Where do your sympathies lie as the drama finishes?

68 What effect is achieved by Leonard Kingston in ending the play the way he does?

General Questions

69 When reading through these plays you probably found yourself, for various personal reasons, identifying with one character or another. If you did, discuss which ones caught your imagination and for what particular reasons.

70 Bearing in mind that they were originally broadcast for schools, which aspects of the plays do you feel are most suited to a classroom audience? Would you recommend any of them to be shown as part of mainstream television output?

71 To what extent do you feel these plays concentrate too heavily on the more depressing side of family life? Do any of the scenes appear as either unrealistic or very true to life? Did you find some parts difficult to visualise and which, you felt, would work much better on the screen than they do on the page?

72 One of the plays has the title *If Only*, and there are many moments in all four dramas where we might think that *if only* someone had acted differently then problems would

not have arisen or situations worsened. Comment on any occasions when you felt that might have been true. What would you have done given the same circumstances? In reading this collection, are you tempted to apportion blame to any of the characters?

*73 Imagine you were given the job of casting director for *one* of the plays. In preparation for auditions, devise portraits (illustrated or written) of each of the characters as you imagine them from reading the text. Compare your descriptions with those done by others in your group – what similarities or striking differences emerge?

*74 *Radio Times* and *TV Times* and our daily newspapers regularly carry previews and reviews of television drama. Try writing your own on any of these four plays, commending them where you think they are good, criticising their weaknesses or where you didn't enjoy them. It would be worth reproducing your reports for other classes to look at if they are reading this volume (of plays).

*75 These plays were, of course, first conceived in visual terms for television and what you have read are scripts edited for classroom reading. Thinking about the television medium, take one particular scene you have enjoyed and attempt to plot in alongside the text camera angles, sound and lighting cues, and the detailed movements of the actors. You could also consider studio sets, props, photo-montages and, where necessary, outside film locations.

A Choice of Books

In reading, one title leads on to another, and we often find most pleasure in picking up a book which in some way or other has been prompted by what we have just read and enjoyed. Listed here is a small choice of books which in various ways touch on similar experiences and ideas to those of the plays in this collection. It would be especially good for members of a group working with this collection each to read a different book from this list and to compare notes later. Groups working on dramatic improvisations or creating their own plays or stories after reading these television scripts will also find the following books helpful comparisons and starting points.

Stories

BANKS, LYNNE REID, *The L-Shaped Room*, Longman (Imprint Books)

BARSTOW, STAN, *A Kind of Loving*, Hutchinson

BARSTOW, STAN, *The Human Element, A Casual Acquaintance*, Longman (Imprint Books)

BECKMAN, GUNNEL, *Mia, Mia Alone*, Longman (Knockouts)

BEHAN, BRENDAN, *Borstal Boy*, Hutchinson

CHAMBERS, AIDAN, editor, *Loving You Loving Me*, Macmillan

CHAPLIN, SID, *The Leaping Lad*, Longman (Imprint Books)

CLEARY, BEVERLY, *Fifteen*, Heinemann

DOUBTFIRE, DIANNE, *This Jim*, Heinemann

DRABBLE, MARGARET, *The Millstone*, Longman (Imprint Books)

DYMENT, CLIFFORD, *The Railway Game*, Dent

HANLEY, CLIFFORD, *A Taste of Too Much*, Blackie

HUDDY, DELIA, *My Kind of Cake*, Macmillan Topliner

KAMM, JOSEPHINE, *Young Mother*, Heinemann

MARLAND, EILEEN and MICHAEL, editors, *Friends and Families*, Longman (Imprint Books)

MARLAND, MICHAEL, editor, *The Experience of Work*, Longman (Imprint Books)

MARLAND, MICHAEL, editor, *The Experience of Love*, Longman (Imprint Books)
MOODY, H.L.B., *Facing Facts*, Blackie
NAUGHTON, BILL, *Late Night on Watling Street*, Longman (Imprint Books)
NAUGHTON, BILL, *One Small Boy*, Longman (Imprint Books)
ROWE, ALBERT, *People Like You*, Faber
REES, DAVID, *The Lighthouse*, Dennis Dobson
SILLITOE, ALAN, *A Sillitoe Selection*, Longman (Imprint Books)
SILLITOE, ALAN, *The Loneliness of the Long-Distance Runner*, and WATERHOUSE, KEITH, *Billy Liar*, Longman (Heritage of Literature Series)
UNWIN, G.G., editor, *A Taste for Living*, Faber
WRIGHT, RICHARD, *Black Boy*, Longman (Imprint Books)

Plays

BARSTOW, STAN, and BRADLEY, ALFRED, *A Kind of Loving*, Blackie
CAMPTON, DAVID, *Laughter and Fear*, Blackie
CHAMBERS, AIDAN, *The Car*, Heinemann
DELANEY, SHELAGH, *A Taste of Honey*, Methuen
DURBAND, ALAN, editor, *Playbill One, Two* and *Three, Prompt One, Two* and *Three*, Hutchinson
HALL, WILLIS, *The Long and the Short and the Tall*, Heinemann
MARLAND, MICHAEL, editor, *Theatre Choice*, Blackie
NAUGHTON, BILL, *Spring and Port Wine*, Heinemann
PLATER, ALAN, *You and Me*, Blackie
RECKFORD, BARRY, *Skyvers*, Penguin
SELF, DAVID, editor, *Working, City Life, Communities, Situation Comedy*, Hutchinson
STORNACH, ALLAN, *Kes* (adapted from Barry Hines's novel) Heinemann
TERSON, PETER, *Zigger-Zagger*, Penguin
WATERHOUSE, KEITH and HALL, WILLIS, *Billy Liar*, Blackie

Television scripts

BARSTOW, STAN, *Joby*, Blackie
GALTON, RAY and SIMPSON, ALAN, *Hancock's Half Hour*, Evans; *Steptoe and Son*, Longman (Imprint Books)
HOPKINS, JOHN, *Talking to a Stranger*, Penguin
JONES, ELWYN, *Sotly, Softly*, Longman (Imprint Books)

JONES, JULIA, *Still Waters*, Longman (Imprint Books)
LEAKE, ALISON, *Juliet Bravo*, Longman (Imprint Books)
MARLAND, MICHAEL, editor, *Scene Scripts One* and *Two, Z cars, Conflicting Generations, The Pressures of Life*, Longman (Imprint Books)
MANVELL, ROGER, *The July Plot*, Blackie
OWEN, ALUN, *Three Television Plays*, Jonathan Cape
OWEN, ALUN, *The Wake* in *Theatre Choice*, Blackie

Radio plays

BRADLEY, ALFRED, editor, *Out of the Air*, Longman (Imprint Books)
BRADLEY, ALFRED, editor, *Worth a Hearing*, Blackie

Acknowledgements

The editor and publisher are grateful to the following for permission to include scripts which are in copyright. Applications for performance rights should be addressed to the authors' agents:

David Cook and Leonard Kingston
c/o Margaret Ramsay Ltd, 14A Goodwin's Court, St Martin's Lane, London WC2N 4LL
David Hopkins
c/o Roger Hancock Ltd, 8 Waterloo Place, Pall Mall, London SWI
Jack Ronder
c/o Fraser and Dunlop Scripts Ltd, 91 Regents Street, London WI

They are also grateful to BBC TV and to the following actors and actresses for permission to reproduce photographs from the television productions of the plays:

Coins Against the Wall – Martin Murphy (David Briars), Vilma Hollingbery (David's mother, Katherine Briars), Patrick Field (Arthur) and Marcus Francis (Mick)
The Kids are Okay – James Morrison (Kenny), Donna McVey (Jill), Mary Riggans (their mother, Mary), Bill Henderson (their father, Andrew), John Murtagh (Kenny's teacher, Mr Mulveen) and Carol Ann Crawford (Andrew's girl friend, Doreen)
If Only – George Winter (Brian) and Simon Chandler (Micky Thompson) *Consequences* – Daniel Abineri (Paul Summers) and Sylvestra le Touzel (Liza Hollander)

The photographs from *If Only* and *Consequences* are copyright the BBC. Those from *Coins Against The Wall* and *The Kids Are Okay* were taken by Terry Williams from video recordings and are copyright Longman Group Ltd.

Longman Imprint Books
General Editor: Michael Marland CBE

Titles in the series

There is a Happy Land Keith Waterhouse
Nine African Stories Doris Lessing
The Experience of Colour *edited by* Michael Marland
* **The Human Element and other stories** Stan Barstow
* **The Leaping Lad and other Stories** Sid Chaplin
Z Cars Four television scripts
Steptoe and Son Four television scripts
Conflicting Generations Five television scripts
* **A Sillitoe Selection** *edited by* Michael Marland
* **Late Night on Watling Street and other stories** Bill Naughton
Black Boy Richard Wright
The Millstone Margaret Drabble
Fair Stood the Wind for France H. E. Bates
Scene Scripts Seven television plays
The Experience of Work *edited by* Michael Marland
Breaking Away *edited by* Marilyn Davies *and* Michael Marland
The Kraken Wakes John Wyndham
A Hemingway Selection *edited by* Dennis Pepper
Friends and Families *edited by* Eileen *and* Michael Marland
Ten Western Stories *edited by* C. E. J. Smith
The Good Corn and other stories H. E. Bates
The Experience of Sport *edited by* John L. Foster
* **Loves, Hopes, and Fears** *edited by* Michael Marland
The African Queen C. S. Forester
* **A Casual Acquaintance and other stories** Stan Barstow
Eight American Stories *edited by* D. L. James
Cider with Rosie Laurie Lee
The L-Shaped Room Lynne Reid Banks
Softly, Softly Five television scripts by Elwyn Jones
The Pressures of Life Four television plays
The Experience of Prison *edited by* David Ball
Saturday Night and Sunday Morning Alan Sillitoe
* **A John Wain Selection** *edited by* Geoffrey Halson
Jack Schaefer and the American West *edited by* C. E. J. Smith
Goalkeepers are Crazy Brian Glanville
A James Joyce Selection *edited by* Richard Adams
Out of the Air Five radio plays, *edited by* Alfred Bradley
Could It Be? *edited by* Michael Marland
The Minority Experience *edited by* Michael Marland *and* Sarah Ray
Scene Scripts Two Five television plays, *edited by* Roy Blatchford
Caribbean Stories *edited by* Michael Marland
An Isherwood Selection *edited by* Geoffrey Halson
A Thomas Hardy Selection *edited by* Geoffrey Halson
While They Fought *edited by* Michael Marland *and* Robin Willcox
The Wave and other stories Liam O'Flaherty
Irish Short Stories *edited by* Frances Crowe
The Experience of Parenthood *edited by* Chris Buckton
The Experience of Love *edited by* Michael Marland
Twelve War Stories *edited by* John L. Foster

The Birds and other stories Daphne du Maurier
A Roald Dahl Selection *edited by* Roy Blatchford
A D. H. Lawrence Selection *edited by* Geoffrey Halson
I'm the King of the Castle Susan Hill
Sliding Leslie Norris
Scene Scripts Three Four television plays, *edited by* Roy Blatchford
Still Waters Three television plays *by* Julia Jones
Comedy Scripts Five television plays, *edited by* Roy Blatchford

* Cassette available